Wonderful Names
of Our
Wonderful Lord

Names and Titles of Jesus Christ
from the Old and New Testaments

Hurlburt & Horton

BARBOUR
PUBLISHING

© 2010 by Barbour Publishing, Inc.

ISBN 978-1-60260-856-6

All scripture quotations, unless otherwise noted, are taken from the King James Version of the Bible.

Scriptures marked ASV are taken from the American Standard Version of the Bible.

Cover image © Bruce Cairns/Trevillion Images

Published by Barbour Publishing, Inc., P.O. Box 719, Uhrichsville, Ohio 44683, www.barbourbooks.com

Our mission is to publish and distribute inspirational products offering exceptional value and biblical encouragement to the masses.

Member of the
Evangelical Christian
Publishers Association

Printed in the United States of America.

*And I will put enmity between thee and the
woman, and between thy seed and her seed.*
GENESIS 3:15

*B*ecause He stooped so low God hath exalted
Him very high" (Philippians 2:9, Arthur Way's
translation). From this first great act and fact in
His revelation to that last greater act when He
died for our sins on Calvary, and up until the
very time when God exalted Him very high to
sit at His own right hand in the heavenlies, our
Savior's example was one of profound humility.
He came from the bosom of the Father to
become the "Seed of the Woman." He turned
from "the words which I have spoken to
you, the same shall judge you," to be in His
innocence judged of sinful men and crucified.
*Oh Lord, You who humbled Yourself to be born of a
woman, who bore our sins in Your own body on the
tree, we bow on our faces before You and worship
and adore. Amen.*

*And the angel of the LORD called unto
Abraham out of heaven the second time.*
GENESIS 22:15

---

*T*he Angel (or Messenger) of Jehovah was
Himself God's message to us. *Oh Lord, You who
Yourself brings Your own message to heal our deep
desolations—You are our sin offering. We praise
You for the glory that You give in our pain by Your
own radiant presence and worship You, oh "Angel of
Jehovah." Amen.*

The sceptre shall not depart from Judah, nor a lawgiver from between his feet, until Shiloh come; and unto him shall the gathering of the people be.

GENESIS 49:10

*I*srael must walk in darkness under law, until the years may seem eternity, but "Shiloh" comes at last and peace. Has Shiloh come to you? And has the peace that passes understanding, the peace *He* made, entered into your soul? For Shiloh came and conquered every foe that could harass you, and stands today offering the peace He made that "passeth knowledge." Have you received it? Has Shiloh come in vain for you? Begin today and "in every thing by prayer and supplication. . .let your requests be made known unto God," and Shiloh's peace shall "keep your heart."

But his bow abode in strength, and the arms of his hands were made strong by the hands of the mighty God of Jacob; (from thence is the shepherd, the stone of Israel).

GENESIS 49:24

Oh "Stone of Israel," Chief Cornerstone, rejected by the builders, Stone of Stumbling, Rock of Offense, Foundation Stone, on which alone we build aught that shall stand, make me a polished, living stone; built in with other stones; perchance a pillar to go out no more, but always a part of Your temple, for Your own indwelling. Thrice-holy Lord, self-offered for my peace; through death that I might live, through fire that I might become indestructible; consumed that I might feed on You in holiest communion—enlighten me today till I perceive Your peace that passes understanding. Amen.

> *And the house of Israel called*
> *the name thereof Manna.*
>
> EXODUS 16:31

There is an art, not known to all who travel, by which a wearied and exhausted life may gather, in a way that seems to those who do not understand almost miraculous, new strength, new vigor, new physical power, for an onward march. So does the Master feed the souls of His children Himself a spiritual "manna" as real and more wonderful than that strange, mysterious food with which He fed the house of Israel. To "feed upon the Lord" may sound like empty mysticism but may be a fact to every trusting soul. For unto us are given "exceeding great and precious promises: that by these [we] might be partakers of the divine nature."

*And when any will offer a meat offering unto the
LORD, his offering shall be of fine flour; and he shall
pour oil upon it, and put frankincense thereon.*
LEVITICUS 2:1

*P*erfect communion with our God as shown in
the "meat offering" was in many senses the highest
pattern that our Savior set for men and women.
Shall we not make it the chiefest plan of every day
to have a time when we enter into such worship
with Him that we may truly say, "There is nothing
between You and me, dear Lord," and then carry
the sweetness of that deep communion unmarred
and uninterrupted through all the hours. *Most
Holy Meal Offering, El Elyon, as You poured upon
the fine meal of Your perfect life the holy oil of Your
most holy Spirit, and the frankincense of Your perfect
adoration, and offer all for me, so I, accepting Yours
that only hallows mine, pour forth my soul, my blood-
cleansed soul, in worship. Holy, holy, holy is the Lord.
Amen.*

The Peace Offering

*And if his oblation be a sacrifice of peace
offering. . .he shall offer it without
blemish before the LORD.*

LEVITICUS 3:1

*I*s there any point of dispute between your Lord
and you? One little thing you do not surrender?
He is right. He cannot change. It is *your* heart
that must surrender. Then you can receive the
peace that passes knowledge. He has made the
offering that atones for all your past, but you must
yield your will to Him. Shall it be now?

*I shall see him, but not now: I shall behold him,
but not nigh: there shall come a Star out of Jacob,
and a Sceptre shall rise out of Israel, and shall smite
the corners of Moab, and destroy all
the children of Sheth.*

NUMBERS 24:17

*W*hat could be more beautiful or more fitting than that our Lord should be called of God a "Star"? Those who know Him best may say, "I shall see him, but not now. I shall behold him, but not nigh." From far beyond our world of trouble and care and change, He shines with undimmed light, a radiant, guiding Star to all who will follow Him—a morning Star, promise of a better day.

A Sceptre shall rise out of Israel.
NUMBERS 24:17

*T*here is a view of Jesus that men and women are slow to see, but someday all the world shall know that a "Sceptre" shall rise out of Israel, and evil will be destroyed before His righteousness more swiftly than ice must melt before the glowing sun. It is in the very nature of things that sin must be consumed before His glorious holiness. Can it be other than the love of sin that blinds the eyes of men and women to His consuming righteousness? *"Search me, O God, and know my heart. Try me and know my thoughts, and see if there be any wicked way in me, and lead me in the way everlasting."* Amen.

The Captain of the Host of the Lord

And he said, Nay; but as captain of the host of the LORD am I now come.

JOSHUA 5:14

The hosts of Israel stand before the gateway to a promised land. No swords are drawn, no skill have they, but with them is an unseen host, and with the host the "Captain of Jehovah's Host." Jericho and all the giants of the land submit, and for you, "behind the dim unknown standeth God within the shadows, keeping watch above His own."

Captain of the hosts of God,
In the path where Thou hast trod,
Bows my soul in humble awe—
Take command. Thy word is law.

Cause me to possess the land,
Led by Thine almighty hand.
Be my guide, defense, and power;
Lead me from this very hour. Amen.

> *The LORD liveth; and blessed be my rock;*
> *and exalted be the God of the rock of my salvation.*
> 2 SAMUEL 22:47

*N*o graver danger threatens believers than that of forgetting that they were redeemed—forgetting even in the joy of realized life what our salvation cost, and what is the rock foundation of our faith. To meet this need our Savior pictures Himself not merely as the Rock of Ages and our Strong Rock of Refuge, but as the *Rock of Our Salvation*. Here, in Him and upon His merit and atoning grace, we were saved from among the lost. Let us glory in this precious name and never forget that He was "wounded for our transgressions" and that he "bore our sins in his own body on the tree."

And he shall be as the light of the morning, when the
sun riseth, even a morning without clouds.
2 SAMUEL 23:4

*N*o single name nor picture of our Lord could possibly reveal Him as the full supply of all our need. Our Lord is to His people not only the "Morning Star," but when the lights of night shall fade in dawning day, He becomes the "Light of the Morning." When all of earth has passed, when all earth's visions fade and flee away, when the great glory of that morning of our eternal life in heaven shall break upon us, we shall find that He who lit all our earthly pilgrimage is still our source of life and guidance over there and will be, to those for whom He has prepared a place, the "Light of the Morning." "So shall we be forever with the Lord."

*And he shall be. . .as the tender grass springing out of
the earth by clear shining after rain.*
2 SAMUEL 23:4

Sheep thrive best in pastures so low and short
that other animals are not able to eat there. The
Good Shepherd leads His flock in pastures where
the tender grass, springing up from the earth after
the rain, brings to them all-sufficient nourishment
as they feed on Him. Oh you who are partakers
of the divine nature, open now the Book of books,
and humbly kneeling, feed on Him who is the
Living Word, the "Tender Grass," which satisfies
and builds up His hungry sheep.

Neither is there any daysman betwixt us,
that might lay his hand upon us both.

JOB 9:33

When the day of reckoning comes, when by all justice I should hear the sentence that my sins deserve, when I shall stand before the Father, stripped of all pretense and sham, then will I fear no evil, for my "Daysman," Mediator, Arbitrator, will stand and speak for me. Can I do less than bow upon my face and worship Him, now and throughout eternity?

But thou, O LORD, art a shield for me; my glory, and the lifter up of mine head.

PSALM 3:3

*T*hat God is "glory"—or "excellence"—beyond our understanding, none can deny. But do our hearts look up to Him today in humble, earnest worship, and know the truth, and speak the truth—"Thou art my Glory"? Our *safety* lies in the fact that He possesses us. Our deepest, holiest *joy* comes only when we humbly say in the hour of secret worship, "Thou art mine." *Oh Lord my Glory, be my shield this day. Amen.*

*But thou, O LORD, art a shield for me; my glory,
and the lifter up of mine head.*

PSALM 3:3

*Oh Thou who hast given
Thy glory to me,
Anoint my blind eyes
Till Thy glory I see.*

*Lift up my bowed head,
Be my shield and my light,
Till Thy radiant glory
Shall banish my night.*

The LORD is my rock, and my fortress, and my deliverer; my God, my strength, in whom I will trust; my buckler, and the horn of my salvation, and my high tower.

PSALM 18:2

A mighty fortress is my God," and no evil may reach the soul that shelters there. There is no saint of God who may look back through all the troubled years of any earthly pilgrimage and not say, if he shall truly speak, "I have been kept by the power of God." Every failure of our lives and each defeat has come when we have sought some earthly fortress rather than our Lord. *I am hiding, Lord, in You. Amen.*

> *But I am a worm, and no man; a reproach of men,*
> *and despised of the people.*
>
> PSALM 22:6

*F*ew harder experiences come to God's children than in these days when those who should be friendly, unjustly make us a reproach, and when they say in the midst of trials that are not the result of any sin in us, "Aha, aha," as though they themselves are righteous, when perchance their sin has brought to us the pain—yet He has walked that way before us. He, too, was a "Reproach of Men"! Shall not the servant walk there, too, and be like Him who in such suffering "opened not his mouth"? *Lord Jesus, who bore scorn and reproach for me, give me the grace of true humility. Amen.*

The LORD is my shepherd; I shall not want.
PSALM 23:1

*T*o say "The Lord is my Shepherd" must carry with it in our understanding not merely grateful praise for the infinite grace and tenderness of the Great Shepherd who leads us by still waters and in green pastures, but confession of our own helplessness and need of a Shepherd's care. And a remembrance also of our lost, undone condition, until

> *All through the mountains, thunder-riven,*
> *And up from the rocky steep,*
> *There arose a glad cry to the gates of heaven,*
> *"Rejoice! I have found My sheep!"*

Lord Jesus, tender Shepherd, lead us forth this day in glad service for You. Amen.

He restoreth my soul: he leadeth me in the paths of righteousness for his name's sake.

PSALM 23:3

*W*e wander from God and from the paths of righteousness—from following Him beside the still waters—till we lose the way, lose joy, lose the sound of His voice. Then the Master "restoreth [the only use of this form in the Old Testament] our soul," "brings us back into his way," into the paths of righteousness. *Oh gracious* Restorer, *bring back my wandering soul as a straying sheep, and lead me on in the paths of righteousness for Your name's sake. Amen.*

Who is the King of glory? Jehovah strong and mighty, Jehovah mighty in battle.
PSALM 24:8 ASV

*I*s your heart faint? Your strength but utter weakness? Behold your Lord—Jehovah—He who reveals Himself as "strong and mighty"—a soldier, a warrior, with sufficient power to break down every opposition. Hear Him say, "My presence shall go with you to conquer every foe." *Strong and mighty Jehovah, give me victory over all the power of the enemy this day. Amen.*

Who is the King of glory? . . . Jehovah mighty in battle.

PSALM 24:8 ASV

*N*o life can be lived for God in these difficult days without terrific conflict. Foes within and foes without assail each saint continuously. Principalities and powers are arrayed against the children of God who seek to serve their Master. We have no might with which to meet "this great host that cometh out against us," but Jehovah, Mighty in Battle, is our Savior, our Intercessor, our Elder Brother, our ever-present Friend. *"Sure, I must fight if I would win; increase my courage, Lord." Amen.*

Who is this King of glory? The LORD of hosts,
he is the King of glory.

PSALM 24:10

*J*ehovah Jesus, the glorious King! Not merely a
king, but glorious, excelling all others in mighty
truth and power, grace and love. We almost forget
for a time His absolute sovereignty as we bow
in humble worship before His matchless glory
and cry again and again, *"Your kingdom come, oh*
glorious King." Amen.

> *Bow down thine ear to me; deliver me speedily:*
> *be thou my strong rock, for an house*
> *of defence to save me.*
>
> PSALM 31:2

*N*o sorrow of men is so deep and dark and bitter as to be without a refuge, a rock, a safe retreat. My soul, however deep your sorrow, however dark your sin, however hopeless your lot among humankind, the Man of Sorrows bore your sin in His own body on the tree. He carried all your grief. He is your "Strong Rock." A strong, safe house, in which I am defended from myself, the world, the devil.

> *Rock of Ages, cleft for me,*
> *Let me hide myself in Thee.*
> *Amen.*

For thou art my rock and my fortress; therefore for thy name's sake lead me, and guide me.
PSALM 31:3

Someday our work shall all be tried by storm and by fire, and the question will be of our foundation. Are we built upon the Rock of Ages, that high Rock that is a Fortress, so that, though the wind blows and the storm shakes all about us, we shall stand secure? And if Christ be our "Rock" and our "Fortress," shall we build with "wood and hay and stubble" upon such an eternal foundation? *Lord Jesus, may we seek to gather "gold and silver and precious stones," that we may bring some honor to You, our Rock and Fortress, by building that which shall endure through all the ages. Amen.*

From the end of the earth will I cry unto thee,
when my heart is overwhelmed: lead me to
the rock that is higher than I.

PSALM 61:2

Not down to a dungeon deep,
Nor to level of earth, hard by—
But lead, when the storm o'erwhelms,
To the "Rock That Is Higher Than I."

Up from my sin's dark slime,
Away from the world's mad cry—
To Thee do I come, O Christ!
To the "Rock That Is Higher Than I."

There will I worship and wait
Redeemed, with the saints on high.
All glory and honor and praise
To the "Rock That Is Higher Than I."

A Strong Tower

For thou hast been a shelter for me, and a strong tower from the enemy.

PSALM 61:3

*W*hat is the testimony of our souls today as we read that which others have said concerning Him who has been a "Strong Tower" from the enemy? Did ever a child of God in danger hasten within the Strong Tower of His presence and find aught of failure or defeat? Must we not confess that every failure has come when we were found outside? *Oh Strong Tower, may we enter in today and dwell in You and be safe.*

*I am become a stranger unto my brethren, and an
alien unto my mother's children.*

PSALM 69:8

*What was the price He paid,
That, what He bore for me;
"A Stranger, an Alien"; alone,
He died on Calvary.*

*A "Stranger" to make me a friend,
An "Alien" to give me a home.
Great Stranger, I fall at Thy feet,
No longer from Thee will I roam.*

Amen.

*Give the king thy judgments, O God, and thy
righteousness unto the king's son.*

PSALM 72:1

*H*ow little do our hearts discern the homage
due to God as King and to Jesus as His Son.
We bow our heads, we lift our hats, we pay our
homage to the fleeting, trifling power of earth's
great men, but do we, as we enter the house of
God, bow humbly and revere the "King's Son"?
Are earthly thoughts hushed and earthly words
stilled as we gather in the house of God, and even
when our spokesman voices our desires to Him,
do wandering thoughts of earthly things deprive
us of the blessing and the answer to our prayers?
*Lord, teach us how to pray, that we may truly worship
You. Amen.*

He shall come down like rain upon the mown grass.
PSALM 72:6

My soul was parched with the fire of sin,
My life mowed down with pain,
My Savior spoke, "My child, draw near."
His word was like the Rain.

Refreshing, cleansing, lifting me,
My Lord, my All, came down,
And now I turn from all earth's dross—
To gain a heavenly crown.

He shall come down like rain upon the mown grass:
as showers that water the earth.

PSALM 72:6

*O*ur lives grow dusty, dry, and desertlike in our
earthly pilgrimage, but He who seeks a love that
is fresh and pure and strong comes down upon us
as "Showers upon the Earth." Have you turned
to Him today and found that cool, refreshing,
cleansing blessing that He seeks to give?

> *There shall be showers of blessing,*
> *Oh, that today they might fall!*
> *Now, as to God we're confessing,*
> *Now, as on Jesus we call.*

Amen.

Also I will make him my firstborn, higher than the kings of the earth.

PSALM 89:27

"Loose thy shoes from off thy feet, for the place where thou standest is holy." The eternal Father, God, is speaking. "My Firstborn I will make higher than the kings of earth." Oh you who are the last-born of the Father, the Firstborn is your Elder Brother. You have shared His humiliation to your salvation. You shall share His exaltation to your eternal glory. *We worship You, Lord Jesus, God's "Firstborn"! Amen.*

> *The stone which the builders refused is become the*
> *head stone of the corner.*
>
> PSALM 118:22

*M*en may reject the "*Head Stone of the Corner*" and seek to erect a building that shall stand without the living Christ. But God has laid aside all human plans and made our Lord and Savior the Head Stone of the Corner. When all human buildings crumble and every man-taught architect has failed, all hearts bow before that perfect building, that eternal temple, worshipping Him who is its crown of grace.

> *My goodness, and my fortress; my high tower, and*
> *my deliverer; my shield, and he in whom I trust;*
> *who subdueth my people under me.*
>
> PSALM 144:2

*M*y High Tower" is a vision of our glorious
Savior as the Most High—high above our trials;
high above our temptations; high above our foes;
high above our failures and losses; high above the
fret and care of our earthward life. A place of holy
calm and peace and stillness. The door is open.
Lord Jesus, our High Tower, let us enter in today.
Amen.

I wisdom dwell with prudence, and find out
knowledge of witty inventions.

PROVERBS 8:12

*W*isdom is the right use of knowledge. What a wondrous name for Him who gave Himself for us! Who, "when he putteth forth his own sheep, goeth before them"; who guides us by the skillfulness of His hand. *May we seek with all our hearts until we find You, and finding You, find wisdom to do the will of God. Amen.*

Let them praise the name of the LORD:
for his name alone is excellent.
PSALM 148:13

"All the glory of the Lord is that in which He excels all others." His name is "Excellent," and all His names that represent some feature of His grace are glorious because they excel any other name ever uttered among men. What friend, what helper do we know on earth who ever has or can approach His excellence? And so we turn with new deep joy to the psalmist's testimony, "They that know thy name will put their trust in thee."

Counsel is mine, and sound wisdom:
I am understanding; I have strength.
PROVERBS 8:14

God is Love, God is Light, God is to us a thousand things for which we long and which we need; but have we realized that in possessing Him and abiding in Him, He is "Understanding," and all that seems dark and difficult will become clear to us as we depend upon Him who is Understanding? It would take ten thousand years to learn a few of the many things we long to know on earth. The soul that is linked to God begins to understand and will go on to clearer understanding throughout the countless ages.

A Friend That Sticketh Closer Than a Brother

*A man that hath friends must shew himself friendly:
and there is a friend that sticketh closer
than a brother.*

PROVERBS 18:24

Stay, lonely pilgrim, searching long for
fellowship. Stop here and find a "Friend." "There
is a Friend," though all the world deny it. One
who is always true and faithful. One who never
leaves and never forsakes. No brother will, or can,
abide as He. Will you be friend to Jesus as He
is a Friend to you? *We worship You; we trust all to
You and take from You all peace, all grace, all needed
power to do and be what pleases You, our never-
absent* Friend. *Amen.*

Because of the savour of thy good ointments thy name is as ointment poured forth.
SONG OF SOLOMON 1:3

Is your soul sore from sin, from chafing, or from the fiery darts of Satan, of sinners, or of saints? Then is your Lord to thee as "Ointment Poured Forth," free, abundant, ready, healing, and fragrant. Suffering soul, come near to Him and let that healing Ointment pour over you and soothe and heal you.

A bundle of myrrh is my well-beloved unto me.
SONG OF SOLOMON 1:13

Oh child of sorrow, Church of Smyrna, sad soul suffocating in earth's dark vapors, your Lord is for you an exquisite perfume, a "Bundle of Myrrh." A missionary, wearily walking a winding pathway in the night, suddenly came upon a spot where the air was heavy with the perfume of wild jasmine and was comforted and refreshed by a fragrance preserved from nonappreciative wild animals and wilder men for a sorrowing toiler. So is your Lord, to you, a "Bundle of Myrrh."

> *My beloved is unto me as a cluster of camphire*
> *in the vineyards of Engedi.*
> Song of Solomon 1:14

A beautiful, fragrant flower—"a cluster" of them—exquisite beauty, exquisite perfume in abundance! Struggling in the midst of experiences that are not fragrant, that are not delightful, have you learned to turn to Him who, in the midst of darkness, is Light; in the midst of battle, is Peace; in the midst of unpleasantness, is to you unlimited and exquisite delight? Do you know your Lord as a "Cluster of Camphire"? Acquaint yourself with Him now, and be at peace.

I am the rose of Sharon.
SONG OF SOLOMON 2:1

Child of God, there is no mood of your life where Jesus fails to fit your need; to brighten as a brilliant rose your life. In joy or sorrow, sunshine or shadow, day or night, He blooms for you. Behold Him, then, today, not only on the cross for you, not only on the throne, but near you, close beside your path, the "Rose of Sharon."

I am. . .the lily of the valleys.
SONG OF SOLOMON 2:1

*S*weetest, fairest, most exquisite flower that eye has seen, hidden save to eyes that seek it out. So does your Lord unveil Himself to you, even though you walk through the valleys. Only in those deeper shadows can you know His utter loveliness. Behold *Him* then, and "fear no evil."

I will rise now, and go about the city in the streets,
and in the broad ways I will seek him
whom my soul loveth.

SONG OF SOLOMON 3:2

Not in the doubting throng,
Not in the boastful song,
But kneeling—with Christ above me—
Humbly I'll say, "I love Thee."

Not with my lips alone,
Not for Thy gifts I own,
But just for the grace I see,
Jesus, my soul loveth Thee.

Amen.

*My beloved is white and ruddy, the chiefest
among ten thousand.*
SONG OF SOLOMON 5:10

*D*o we sometimes sing with too little depth of
meaning "He's the chiefest of ten thousand to my
soul"? Is He really first in our hearts' affection?
If so, His presence has been real to us, for He has
said, "Ye shall seek me, and find me, when ye shall
search for me with all your heart," or "with your
whole desire." Here the secret of full transforming
communion with our Lord Jesus Christ is found
in gazing upon Him in all the beauty of His
holiness, until in very truth He becomes in our
hearts the "Chiefest among Ten Thousand."

His mouth is most sweet: yea, he is altogether lovely.
SONG OF SOLOMON 5:16

Every earthly joy will pall,
Every earthly friend will fall.
Only Christ is to the end
"Altogether Lovely," friend.

Do you see His wondrous face
Full of glory, love, and grace?
Look, and all thy need confess;
Worship His pure holiness.

In that day shall the branch of the LORD
be beautiful and glorious.

ISAIAH 4:2

*B*y every means and picture that we can
understand, the Spirit reveals our Savior's oneness
with God. None is clearer or fuller of meaning to
us than this, the "Branch of the Lord." One with
the Father, growing out of and yet a part of Him.
And we are "branches" of Christ (see John 15). As
we worship the Christ who is very God, we hear
Him say, "If ye abide in me. . .ye shall ask what ye
will, and it shall be done unto you."

*And one cried unto another, and said, Holy,
holy, holy, is Jehovah of hosts: the
whole earth is full of his glory.*

ISAIAH 6:3 ASV

The "Jehovah" of the Old Testament is the
"Jesus" of the New. If we always think (as Scofield
suggested) of Jehovah as "God revealing Himself,"
and the words of Jehovah-Jesus, "Blessed are the
pure in heart: for they shall see God," then shall
the heavens about us be always full of the chariots
and horsemen of Jehovah of Hosts, and all fear
shall be stilled and His revelation of Himself to us
will not be in vain. *Lord Jesus, Jehovah of Hosts, give
us a vision of Your glory this day. Amen.*

For before the child shall know to refuse the evil, and choose the good, the land that thou abhorrest shall be forsaken of both her kings.

ISAIAH 7:16

*T*he first, last, and chiefest mark of Christ's deity was His great humility. The greatest Sage and Seer of all the ages, a "Child"! The everlasting God, hoary-white with eternal years, a "Child"! Then shall we hesitate to "become as little children," knowing that only so shall we enter the kingdom?

And he shall be for a sanctuary.

ISAIAH 8:14

*W*here is your place of worship? Where, in the turmoil of the street; where, in the busy cares of home; where, in the hurry and confusion of humankind, shall our souls find the place to pray? "He shall be for a sanctuary, closer to thee than breathing, nearer than hands or feet." At any moment during all the hurried day you may be hidden from all earth's eyes, and still from all earth's din. Only abide in Him.

A Great Light

*The people that walked in darkness have seen a great
light: they that dwell in the land of the shadow of
death, upon them hath the light shined.*

ISAIAH 9:2

It is the people who once walked in darkness
who are able to see the greatness of the light. It
is the soul that finds it is lost that seeks the Lord.
Have you seen the Light? The beloved apostle
said, "That which we have seen, declare we unto
you, and this is the message that we declare
unto you, that God is Light, and in him is no
darkness." *Lord, let my life and lips tell out the story
of the Light my eyes have seen. Amen.*

> *For unto us a child is born, unto us a son is given. . .and his name shall be called Wonderful.*
> ISAIAH 9:6

*J*esus is "the same yesterday, today, and forever," and men and women who think Him commonplace or at most only an unusual man will sometime stand ashamed and confounded as they hear this prophecy fulfilled, "His name shall be called Wonderful." Today He is working just as wonderful works as when He created the heaven and the earth. His wondrous grace, His wonderful omnipotence, is for His child who needs Him and who trusts Him, even today. Attempt great things for God and expect great things from Him, and you will begin even now to say, "His name is Wonderful."

*For unto us a child is born, unto us a son is
given. . .and his name shall be called. . .Counsellor.*
ISAIAH 9:6

*N*ot often is He called "Counsellor" now. Even
God's saints continuously ask of mere humans
instead of God, "How may I find God's will?"
Conference after conference is held by both the
world and the church to find by human wisdom
some better plan for earthly government, or for
the church, or for the welfare of our earthly life
and walk. But how rarely do we bow together or
alone to seek that heavenly wisdom, that divine
counsel that alone will enable us to find our way
out of the mazes in which we wander. When
shall His name be joyfully and triumphantly
proclaimed as "Counsellor" by His people? By
you?

For unto us a child is born, unto us a son is given. . .and his name shall be called. . . The mighty God.

ISAIAH 9:6

*H*ave we doubted His might and feared in the day when some foe was near? Hark! His name is the "Mighty God." Then away with all doubt and fear! "Thou hast made both the heaven and earth. There is nothing too hard for thee." Lord, I bow to the dust and worship. *Mighty God, show Your power in me! Amen.*

For unto us a child is born, unto us a son is given. . .and his name shall be called. . . The everlasting Father.

ISAIAH 9:6

*W*ho has not mourned a father's death and felt the loss of his transient power and helpfulness? The Child who was born in Bethlehem, who gave His life for you, is not alone your Savior and your King, but His name shall be called the *"Everlasting Father."* In His everlasting love, within His everlasting arms, within His Father-heart that pities you, His child, you shall find safety, rest, and comfort.

For unto us a child is born, unto us a son is given. . .and his name shall be called. . .
The Prince of Peace.

ISAIAH 9:6

*H*e who proclaimed to loyal hearts, "My peace I leave with you. My peace I give unto you. Not as the world giveth give I unto you," is rightly called the "Prince of Peace." He who brought such peace to earth was rejected of men and women and waits still to be crowned on earth; but He gives before that royal day a peace that passes understanding to every trusting heart. Have you received it? Will you, in loyalty to the "Prince of Peace," accept in humble faith His peace today?

> *And the light of Israel shall be for a fire, and his*
> *Holy One for a flame: and it shall burn and devour*
> *his thorns and his briers in one day.*
> ISAIAH 10:17

*J*esus was and is the "Light of Israel." He is
also the "Light of life" and the "Light of men," a
"Light to lighten world." But the "Light of
Israel" was "to burn and devour thorns and briers."
Dear child of God, are you bringing the useless
branches, the unpleasant, unlovely things of your
life, into the Light of His presence, that they
may be consumed? Someday the shining of His
presence will destroy the very Advocate of evil.
Shall we not submit our lives to that wondrous
Light and ask Him to consume all evil in us?

And there shall come forth a rod out of the stem of Jesse, and a Branch shall grow out of his roots.
ISAIAH 11:1

Only a "rod" from a human "stem"? Only a "root" from "dry ground"? Has He no "form nor comeliness," no "beauty that we should desire"? Surely He bore our griefs, and the way of our peace was in Him. "Because He stooped so low God hath exalted Him very high," and the comeliness of a tender plant was the glory of God on high.

And a Branch shall grow out of his roots.
ISAIAH 11:1

*O*f all the miracles that attest to the deity of our Lord, including the miraculous preservation of the Scriptures, none is more wonderful or convincing to the honest, faithful heart than the preservation, not only of Israel, but of that section of Israel, humble in its origin, that revealed our Lord to be born of the family of David and of Jesse. Out of the nations scattered over the earth, out of the line of kings who long had ceased to reign, there came forth, as the prophet said, a "Branch out of His Roots" of the stem of Jesse. And He who was of the seed of David shall just as surely come again to reign once more over Israel, and through Israel over all the earth. *Lord, our faint hearts believe anew in God's eternal truth and faithfulness. Amen.*

And in that day there shall be a root of Jesse. . . .to it shall the Gentiles seek: and his rest shall be glorious.
ISAIAH 11:10

*I*t is not Israel alone who shall rejoice when "a root of Jesse. . .shall stand for an ensign of the people," for "to it shall the Gentiles seek," and all the gracious promises and gifts God gave to Jesse and to David and his seed that could bring rest and comfort to our souls belong to us who worship Jesus, David's Son and Jesse's Root. How all the grace and glory of our God through all the ages are gathered up for us who from the Gentile world bow at His feet and find His glorious rest!

And in that day there shall be a root of Jesse, which shall stand for an ensign of the people; to it shall the Gentiles seek: and his rest shall be glorious.

ISAIAH 11:10

*J*esus is the people's flag, an "Ensign of the People." Wherever and whenever He is lifted up, the people seek after Him. Is not our failure to win many to the Lord due to our misrepresentation of Him? To our failure to reveal the beauty of His holiness and to enter into His glorious rest? Shall we bow in humble confession while we pray that we who are His representatives may be saved from misrepresentation of Him by lives that are cruelly unlike Him and seek for grace to exalt Him everywhere among men and women?

Behold, God is my salvation; I will trust, and not be afraid: for the LORD JEHOVAH is my strength and my song; he also is become my salvation.

ISAIAH 12:2

*W*e know Jehovah is our "Strength," but do we make Him also our "Song"? As we make Him so and sing of Him, we lose our fear. We are able to "trust and not be afraid" only as we sing of Him. Our Redeemer is our Strength. Make Him your Song today.

And I will fasten him as a nail in a sure place; and he shall be for a glorious throne to his father's house.
ISAIAH 22:23

*M*en have dreamed fantastic ideas concerning Christ as a "Nail in a Sure Place." Whatever else this name may or may not mean, it brings to the worshipping child of God a sense of the fixedness, the certainty and security of Jesus Christ in His relationship to the temple and throne of God. If we on earth are being built together for a habitation of God, yet surer is the fact of the presence of Christ filling the house. If we are "pillars who go no more out," it is because He is secure—His place is "fastened" and "sure." "So shall we ever be with the Lord," for where He is, there shall also His servant be, and our abiding is as sure as Christ's.

*And he shall be for a glorious throne
to his father's house.*

ISAIAH 22:23

*O*ne of the most vivid pictures painted by the
Holy Spirit of the life that lies beyond follows
in the Revelation—the swift, wondrous vision of
the church on earth (Revelation 4:2–3). "Behold,
a throne was set in heaven. . .and there was a
rainbow round about the throne." That rainbow
brings us hope and comfort and the precious,
glorious promise that our Lord Himself is a
"Glorious Throne to His Father's House." Let it
be no longer hard or difficult for you to pray. The
throne before which you bow is not one of austere
justice but rather one of infinite grace. Let us
therefore come boldly to the throne of grace, that
we may obtain mercy and find help.

> *For thou hast been a strength to the poor,*
> *a strength to the needy in his distress.*
> ISAIAH 25:4

*T*ouched with the feeling of our infirmities,
our Lord in His omnipotence becomes a
"Strength to the Poor and Needy." Let us never
forget that His strength is made perfect in our
weakness only when we realize our helplessness
and fling ourselves, as trusting children, into
the outstretched arms by which He "created the
heavens and the earth." With what a wondrous
picture does our Lord reveal Himself as the supply
for our every need and as a strength to the poor!

For thou hast been. . .a shadow from the heat.
ISAIAH 25:4

*I*n the intolerable heat of the sun as it beats
upon the plateaus of equatorial Africa, one may
step from the unbearable heat to a shade so
cool, so refreshing, that until it is experienced
it is almost beyond conception or belief. Thus
our Lord pictures Himself to His weary, toiling
children, struggling onward in the heat of almost
impossible experiences, as a "*Shadow from the
Heat*," into whose presence we may step at
any moment of our pilgrimage and find cool,
refreshing rest.

For thou hast been. . .a refuge from the storm. . .when the blast of the terrible ones is as a storm against the wall.

ISAIAH 25:4

*G*od is faithful, who will not suffer you to be tempted above that ye are able; but will with the temptation also make a way to escape," a "refuge from the storm," "that ye may be able to bear it." It needs must be that we pass through storms and that we feel their force and chilling blast, for only in such experiences could we ever know the comfort, the witness, of Him who is our *"Refuge from the Storm."* Are we hiding in Him?

Trust ye in Jehovah for ever; for in Jehovah,
even Jehovah, is an everlasting rock.
[Margin, "rock of ages."]

ISAIAH 26:4 ASV

*M*any of the college buildings at Oxford
University, hundreds of years old, were described
by one who studied there more than half a
century ago as "leprous with age." Many stones
are crumbling away, and some must be replaced
to save the buildings. The strongest rocks in
which men hide the bodies of departed friends are
ofttimes riven by a growing plant. But He who
calls us to "trust in Jehovah forever" calls Himself
an *"Everlasting Rock"* or the *"Rock of Ages."* Let us
trust in Him today, tomorrow, and forever.

In that day shall the LORD of hosts be for a crown of glory. . .unto the residue of his people.

ISAIAH 28:5

*W*e hear and think much of redeemed and fruitful saints shining as stars in the diadem of our Lord, but in this wondrous title of our glorious Savior we have a new vision of His relationship to His people. Souls who have been downtrodden and scorned by those whom the world calls great will in that day, as He honors redeemed believers as His Bride, find that the presence, the tender and gracious love of the King of Glory, will be to them in the eyes of all a witness, a "Crown of Glory." Oh you who are redeemed from among the lost, you who were dead and are alive, were lost and are found, behold His wondrous grace! The King of kings, the Lord of lords, shall be to you a Crown of Glory. Then fall at His feet today and worship Him with all your heart.

In that day shall the LORD of hosts be for. . .a diadem of beauty, unto the residue of his people.
ISAIAH 28:5

The difference between a "crown of glory" and a "diadem of beauty" is that in the first the excellence, the worth, the value, the glory of God shall be upon the saints. While in the other, the beauty, the very radiance of the Lord, shall fill and shine out from those who, in a moment, in the twinkling of an eye, shall be changed into His likeness. Oh humble child of God, behold the exceeding grace that shall be revealed in the ages to come. The beauty of the Lord our God shall be upon you, and He shall be to you a crown or "Diadem of Beauty." "He that hath this hope in him purifieth himself."

Therefore thus saith the Lord GOD, Behold, I lay in Zion for a foundation a stone.

ISAIAH 28:16

Of all the gracious promises concerning the children of God, none is more wonderful than that which describes the saints as polished stones in the temple where He dwells. With divine grace our Lord calls Himself the "Foundation," an "Everlasting Rock," the "Rock of Ages." Where stands our faith today? Are we building upon the sands of human philosophies or upon Him?

> *On the Rock of Ages founded,*
> *Naught can shake our sure repose.*

Therefore thus saith the Lord GOD, Behold, I lay in Zion. . .a sure foundation.

ISAIAH 28:16

All the chiseling, all the polishing of experiences through which we pass, is costly. Will it last? Is it worthwhile? Worthwhile to suffer on and say, "Dear Lord, stay not Your hand to comfort us and steady us"? Through just such testing times the Master calls Himself a *"Sure Foundation."* No experiment here, no doubt, no room for anxious thought or fear. Those who build upon that "Sure Foundation" find their building sure, and they shall be "pillars in the temple of God," to "go no more out" forever.

A Tried Stone

Therefore thus saith the Lord GOD, Behold, I lay in Zion for a foundation a stone, a tried stone, a precious corner stone.

ISAIAH 28:16

*H*ow strange is this experience of our Lord. Surely the Father knew the Son, knew His every capacity and power. Yet He was tried of God as we have need to be tried, only that He might "leave us an example," that we might walk in His steps. What mockery, what hopeless blasphemy, that He should be rejected by some builders! Let us bid the great Master Builder to try us and to chisel us until we fit in the place that He has prepared for us.

And a man shall be as. . .a covert from the tempest.
ISAIAH 32:2

Of no other being could such language be used, in no other literature of the world is such marvelous imagery to be found, as that used in the Word of God to picture the grace and glory of our Lord. When the destructive tempests sweep and we hide in Him, shall we be safe? He shall be a *"Covert from the Tempest"*—covered, sheltered, safe. Are we hiding in Him?

And a man shall be as an hiding place from the wind.
ISAIAH 32:2

Standing one day on the deck of a steamer in the harbor at Aden, a traveler saw a storm of wind sweeping across the desert like some high, mountainous wave, rolling and sweeping forward until it struck the sea and lashed it to foam. Then on across the bay until it struck ships lying there at anchor, till nearly every boat was torn from its moorings or forced to loosen every cable and steam with full force into the face of the terrific wind. No hiding place was there. So do the storms of hate, of evil, and of sin sweep over our lives as we journey toward our everlasting home. But for every soul who knows his or her own helplessness, our Savior is Himself a "Hiding Place from the Wind."

And a man shall be as. . .the shadow of a great rock in a weary land.

ISAIAH 32:2

Journeying one night in the wilderness of central Africa in a section plagued by many ravenous beasts, we found no place of safety till we came to the shadow of a great rock, where we sat down with our backs to the rock and, building at our feet a great fire, found rest and refreshing for the next day's still weary journey. Oh weary child, when your strength fails and you can go no farther, sit down and lean back in the shadow of your Lord, upon Him. Build there in prayer the fire of faith and find rest and refreshment for your onward march.

> *And a man shall be as. . .rivers of water*
> *in a dry place.*
>
> ISAIAH 32:2

To know the blessing of water in abundance, we need to have felt a very keen thirst. Wandering one time in part of Africa's desert, two missionaries traveled without water until thirst became first a pain, then an agony, then almost insanity. After long marching over dry, burning sands, they came to the waters of a wide, deep river and quenched their thirst. "If any man thirst, let him come unto me," and He is near. No matter how deep our thirst, how great our longing or our need, He who is as *"Rivers of Water in a Dry Place"* has said, "Lo, I am with you. Drink, and be satisfied."

> *Thine eyes shall see the king in his beauty: they shall behold the land that is very far off.*
>
> ISAIAH 33:17

*B*lessed are the pure in heart, for they shall see God." Do our lives see the King in His beauty? Do we grip the fact that as we gaze upon Him, it is His will that we should be changed unto the same likeness, "from glory unto glory"? "A little while and the world seeth me no more, but ye see me." No more wonderful promise is ours for present experiences than this. Oh Lord, let every mist and veil that hide Your glory be removed, and every sin be put away, that we may behold You in the beauty of holiness. Then "the beauty of the Lord thy God shall be upon thee."

> *For the LORD is our judge, the LORD is our lawgiver,*
> *the LORD is our king; he will save us.*
>   ISAIAH 33:22

*E*very nation, every act, every life needs a law to direct it in its relation to its own expression and to others. That law must be made by one who knows and understands the nation, act, or life. Jesus is our "Lawgiver." He who gave us life, He who has lived the life we need to live—He knows. He made the law for us in infinite tenderness and love. "He that hath my commandments, and keepeth them, he it is that loveth me."

The voice of one that crieth, Prepare ye in the wilderness the way of Jehovah; make level in the desert a highway for our God.

ISAIAH 40:3 ASV

*J*ehovah—the Self-Existent One who reveals Himself." Into the wilderness of my lost way He comes to find me and lead me out. Into the desert of my barren life enters Jehovah and makes all the desert a garden. Into my death He brings His life and to my dead senses reveals Himself the one eternal God. Shall we not bow before His majesty and worship Jehovah, while we pray for greater grace to receive all the revelation of Himself that He would give?

Behold, the Lord Jehovah will come as a mighty one,
and his arm will rule for him: Behold, his reward is
with him, and his recompense before him.

ISAIAH 40:10 ASV

Not every soul who worships Jehovah has
learned that the secret of all power and of fullness
of blessing is in making Him the Master of our
lives. Adonai Jehovah is the Lord, the Ruler, the
Master who in eternal grace reveals Himself. Shall
we not humbly bow at His feet and crown Him
Lord, Master of all that we have and are?

Hast thou not known? hast thou not heard, that the everlasting God, the LORD, the Creator of the ends of the earth, fainteth not, neither is weary? there is no searching of his understanding.

ISAIAH 40:28

Everlasting, never-ending,
Age-abiding is my Lord.
Never shadow caused by turning,
Changeless, perfect, is His Word.

Everlasting God, I pray Thee
Steady, strengthen, stablish me.
Safe from grief and pain and failure,
Hide me, everlasting God, in Thee.

Behold my servant, whom I uphold; mine elect, in whom my soul delighteth; I have put my spirit upon him: he shall bring forth judgment to the Gentiles.
ISAIAH 42:1

Infinite God, who knows and understands, the God of wisdom and of knowledge, called in review all angels and all people of all the ages and of all time and chose our Lord and called Him "Mine Elect," to be the world's Redeemer, Savior, Friend, and the believer's All in All. Does your choice fall on Him each day, each hour, in each experience? May He be all in all to you today.

I the LORD have called thee in righteousness, and will. . .give thee. . .for a light of the Gentiles.
ISAIAH 42:6

*I*n him was life, and the life was the light of men." But how shall that Light lighten the Gentiles unless we who are the light of the world shall go forth among the Gentiles and let the Light shine? Someone brought that Light to us. Shall we not bear it on a little farther into the darkness of some other life? He *is* the Light. He *gave* the Light. *We* are the *Light-bearers.*

The Polished Shaft

And he hath made my mouth like a sharp sword;
in the shadow of his hand hath he hid me,
and made me a polished shaft.

ISAIAH 49:2

*I*n every part of the Word of God our Lord is pictured as the "Word of God" having a "voice as the sound of many waters" and speaking to His people words of peace and comfort and of power. But no name of Christ is truer of Him than that He is a *"Polished Shaft,"* and when He speaks and His word cuts through our selfish lives like a sword of radiant light, let us rejoice. The Adversary of our souls would make us proud of self. Few human friends are faithful, but He who is a "Polished Shaft" speaks not only with eternal love but with unchanging faithfulness. *"Speak, Lord, for thy servant heareth thee."* Amen.

*Thus saith the LORD, the Redeemer of Israel, and
his Holy One, to him whom man despiseth, to him
whom the nation abhorreth, to a servant of rulers,
Kings shall see and arise, princes also shall worship,
because of the LORD that is faithful, and the Holy
One of Israel, and he shall choose thee.*

ISAIAH 49:7

All Israel walked in sin. All Israel was defiled.
And yet in cloud by day, in fire by night, within
the holy tabernacle there stood a Presence, holy,
infinite in love and grace and power. The "*Holy
One of Israel*" could not forget His chosen people
nor resist their faintest cry. So Israel stood and
lived, and lives today because the "Holy One of
Israel" stood beside them. And beside your soul
He stands today to be your righteousness and lead
you to Himself. Behold Him, and adore!

A Root out of a Dry Ground

For he shall grow up before him as a tender plant,
and as a root out of a dry ground.

ISAIAH 53:2

Dear discouraged soul, does it seem sometimes to you that your lot is a hard one? That you have been asked to stand in difficult places and where surrounding conditions have been most unfavorable? He who redeemed you knows every difficulty, every sorrow that you can feel. Dishonored by ignorant doubters, He turned even to the wondrous mother who had received both natural and supernatural knowledge of His divine character and mission and asked, "How is it that ye sought me? Wist ye not. . . ?" He has suffered "in all points like as we" and is, therefore, "able to succor" us. Then consider him who grew up a "Root Out of a Dry Ground," lest ye grow weary and faint in your minds.

A Man of Sorrows

*He is despised and rejected of men; a man of sorrows,
and acquainted with grief: and we hid as it
were our faces from him; he was despised,
and we esteemed him not.*

ISAIAH 53:3

*H*e who was the source of all joy, the giver of
all peace, He before whom angels and archangels
bow in adoration, is also called a "Man of
Sorrows." Grief broke His heart, crushed out His
life. Shall we through disobedience, rebellion,
or lack of love or service or worship add to the
sorrows that He bore, or shall we murmur if we,
too, shall be permitted to partake of His sorrows
or to share His grief? He sorrowed all alone,
save perhaps as angels ministered to Him in
Gethsemane's deep shadow. But He shares your
grief; He carries all your sorrow and comforts
those who trust in Him. Shall we not worship and
adore the *Man of Sorrows*?

He shall see of the travail of his soul, and shall be satisfied: by his knowledge shall my righteous servant justify many; for he shall bear their iniquities.

ISAIAH 53:11

*T*here are many servants; only One is righteous. Paul was able to say, "I have declared unto you the whole counsel of God, I have fought a good fight, I have kept the faith," but still must call himself an unprofitable servant, and less than the least of all saints. Shall we therefore become discouraged and conclude that it is not worthwhile to try? No, "your labor is not in vain in the Lord," for He who was God's "Righteous Servant" shall justify many. For He is still "Jehovah Tsidkenu" (our Righteousness), and we may bring the dropped stitches of our best weaving, and the broken efforts of our best service, and laying all at His feet rejoice that we are justified by Him who is God's Righteous Servant.

For thy Maker is thine husband.

ISAIAH 54:5

*W*e hear of "self-made individuals," of people who are made by their surroundings or by devoted friends and fellows. How rarely do we hear today the humble, joyful boast, "By the grace of God I am what I am." And yet He is your Maker! All you are that is lasting, all you are that is good, all you are that is helpful, God has made. Bow, then, before your Maker. Worship and petition Him to finish that which He began.

The LORD of hosts is his name; and thy Redeemer
the Holy One of Israel; The God of the whole
earth shall he be called.

ISAIAH 54:5

Is there any part of the earth that is mine? Not
till I am truly a child of the "God of the Whole
Earth." May I not receive Him and possess all
things in Christ and proceed to enjoy them,
untroubled by the world's woe? Not till the whole
earth has heard that He is the God, not of a few,
but "of the whole earth."

Behold, I have given him for a witness to the people.
ISAIAH 55:4

A witness of the love of God, the grace, the power, the holiness of deity. No flaw in all that matchless testimony, no doubtful, double-meaning speech, and He could say, "He that hath seen me hath seen the Father." We, too, are witnesses, but oh, how full of flaws is all our testimony! The Father dwelled with Him, and He sought the Father's guidance at every step and every word. We, too, may see and hear and walk with God, and so alone shall our witness win the wanderers home.

A Leader

Behold, I have given him for. . .a leader and commander to the people.

ISAIAH 55:4

From the beginning of our Christian lives the fact that "He leadeth me" is one of the most blessed thoughts that comes to a child of God. But we think most often of His leading to battle, leading out of the mazes of confusion and ignorance, leading through the darkness of our night. Do we realize that infinite tenderness that makes Him gently lead those who are doing the finest and the most difficult and unknown service of the world? The sorrow, the loneliness, the pain that no friend on earth can know, He understands, He feels with us, and gently leads us through the shadows to His own great glory. Shall we not follow where He leads and keep so close to Him that we shall never miss the way?

> *Behold, I have given him for a. . .*
> *commander to the people.*
>
> ISAIAH 55:4

*I*n a day when nearly every man desires to do that which is right in his own eyes, it becomes difficult for all God's children to recognize His right to command. Yet He who redeemed us, who bought us so that we are not our own, proclaimed His right to the title of "Commander." Failure to obey will account for most of the loss of communion and joy in prayer and in the study of God's Word. If there be any commandment that He has brought home to our hearts that we have not obeyed, shall we not today grant Him instant, cheerful, loving obedience, and make Him in every detail of life our Commander?

The Redeemer

*And the Redeemer shall come to Zion, and unto them
that turn from transgression in Jacob, saith the LORD.*
ISAIAH 59:20

*W*hen failure comes and disappointment, when
your soul has been defeated and the race seems
hopeless, stop and think, "Thy Lord redeemed
thee and at countless cost." If He saw in you that
for which to pay His life, Himself, His all, is it
not worthwhile to rise and try again, walking with
Him and worshipping Him who redeemed you?

Thy sun shall no more go down; neither shall thy moon withdraw itself: for the LORD shall be thine everlasting light, and the days of thy mourning shall be ended.

ISAIAH 60:20

No picture is more difficult for us to spiritually apprehend than a time when the sun shall no more go down. When Christ shall be to us "Everlasting Light." Our lives are so filled with ups and downs, with lights and shadows, that stability seems almost inconceivable, and everlasting darkness easier to understand than everlasting light. Yet such is Christ to you. Then enter in with holy boldness and walk in Everlasting Light.

In all their affliction he was afflicted, and the angel of his presence saved them: in his love and in his pity he redeemed them; and he bare them, and carried them all the days of old.

ISAIAH 63:9

A nervous, restless boy, in his early childhood, called out again and again in the night, "Daddy, are you there?" The father answered, "Yes, I am here. Do you want anything?" "No, I only wanted to be sure you were there." And the frightened boy, still in the dark, went directly to sleep. Oh child of God, beset by fears and troubled so that you have found no rest, let the "Angel of His Presence" comfort you. Unstop your ears. Speak to Him, and you shall hear the voice of Him who spoke as never man spoke, saying, "Lo, I am with you."

But now, O LORD, thou art our father; we are
the clay, and thou our potter; and we
all are the work of thy hand.

ISAIAH 64:8

*H*ave you understood the meaning of the force
that presses in upon your life today? Has it seemed
only pain, only wrong and deep injustice? Back
of all that seems to be, the Potter *stands*, with an
ideal so lofty that our highest imagination has not
fully grasped it. A beauteous, transformed life, fit
to sit with Him upon His throne, is in the Potter's
mind, and He is shaping you through that which
seemed a rude experience. Shall we not learn to
say today, "*I am the clay, and You* the Potter. *Shape*
me as You will, dear Lord." Amen.

Is there no balm in Gilead?
JEREMIAH 8:22

There are experiences of suffering through which the Master wills that we should pass. There are burdens that He does not lift, though He takes us, burden and all, into His everlasting arms. But in every suffering that He permits, He is our "Balm." He eases every pain. He comforts every sorrow. He strengthens us in every weakness. There is a "Balm" in our Gilead. Shall we take from Him the comfort that He offers us today?

My Physician

Is there no balm in Gilead; is there no physician there? Why then is not the health of the daughter of my people recovered?

JEREMIAH 8:22

*D*r. Arthur T. Pierson once said in a sermon preached in London, England, that one of the marked proofs of our failure to live up to the light we have is found in our failure to obey the commandment in James's epistle, "Is any sick among you? Let him call for the elders of the church, and let them pray over him." We rush at once to secure human aid, forgetting even to pray as we go, or that He who formed us and through whose blessing alone the human means can be effective is our "Physician."

The portion of Jacob is not like them: for he is the former of all things; and Israel is the rod of his inheritance: The LORD of hosts is his name.
JEREMIAH 10:16

*W*hen we are able to lay hold of the fact that Jesus is our "Portion," then do we truly possess all things, for "how shall he not with him freely give us all things?" No, more: "For all things are yours. Whether Paul, or Apollos, or Cephas, or the world, or life, or death, or things present, or things to come, all are yours. And ye are Christ's, and Christ is God's." Shall we seek to appropriate all of His matchless love and grace and hope and courage and joy and fruit and power? What more can we ask or have?

> *O the hope of Israel, the saviour thereof in time of trouble, why shouldest thou be as a stranger in the land, and as a wayfaring man that turneth aside to tarry for a night?*
>
> JEREMIAH 14:8

The "Hope of His People," Israel, is also the Hope of His Bride, the church. Israel shall be regathered and become, though now despised of man and all nations, the chiefest kingdom in all the earth. And when He shall come, He shall be both "Hope" and full fruition to every believing soul. *"Even so come, Lord Jesus, come quickly."* Amen.

A Righteous Branch

Behold, the days come, saith the LORD, that I will raise unto David a righteous Branch, and a King shall reign and prosper, and shall execute judgment and justice in the earth.

JEREMIAH 23:5

A "righteous servant" is one who serves righteously, satisfying every command of his master. A "righteous branch" is one that rightly respects, honors, and bears fruit to the tree from which it grows. "Ye are branches," our Savior said of us, but He also said, "My Father pruneth." He who is the Righteous Branch heard the Father say, "This is my beloved Son in whom I am well pleased." Shall we not seek with all our hearts to so abide in Him that we shall glorify the Father by bearing much fruit?

> *But they shall serve the LORD their God, and David*
> *their king, whom I will raise up unto them.*
> JEREMIAH 30:9

*W*hat doubt, what incredulity of humankind has blinded human eyes lest they should see that David, Israel's King, shall truly be raised up unto them! How much we lose of deep reality, of wondrous truth and vivid picture in the Word of God, because our eyes are clouded by our unbelief. How beautiful, how wonderful, that Christ our coming Lord should call Himself "David, Their King." What are our thoughts and prayers concerning Israel? Are we seeking, hoping for their King and telling them that He is our King, too? And praying that their eyes may be anointed to behold in Christ "David, Their King"!

Resting Place

*My people hath been lost sheep: their shepherds have
caused them to go astray, they have turned them away
on the mountains: they have gone from mountain to
hill, they have forgotten their restingplace.*

JEREMIAH 50:6

Truly there is rest for the weary, for Jesus is our
"Resting Place." Therefore, in the midst of the
toil and the weariness, in the midst of the struggle
and strife, let us ask that our ears may be opened
to hear Him who said, "Come unto me, all ye
who labour and are heavy laden, and I will give
you rest." To abide in Him in continuous love and
obedient faith is to find Him our Resting Place.

And I will set up one shepherd over them. . .and he shall be their shepherd.

EZEKIEL 34:23

Is any name more comforting to weary, needy children of our God than Jesus' name of "Shepherd"? Feeding, leading beside still water, watching over all our wanderings, bringing us as the Shepherd of Israel brought His flock out of the wilderness over the Jordan into the land of peace and plenty. Teach us to trust in You, oh Shepherd of Israel. Amen.

> *And I will set up one shepherd over them, and he shall feed them, even my servant David; he shall feed them, and he shall be their shepherd.*
>
> EZEKIEL 34:23

*T*he lie of the Adversary to God's children is always that they are "lost." Or that "difficulty is a sign that God has ceased to know or care." When we have wandered from Him, from right, from rest, from peace, "He restoreth my soul." It is His self-appointed task—the work that love makes a necessity for Him, as well as for His wandering sheep.

> *How gentle God's commands,*
> *How kind His precepts are.*

What He feeds is as important for us to learn as when and where. So let us cultivate our appetite, our longing, for His righteousness, and we shall find He is our "Feeder."

> *And I will raise up for them a plant of renown,*
> *and they shall be no more consumed with*
> *hunger in the land, neither bear the*
> *shame of the heathen any more.*
>
> EZEKIEL 34:29

Although our Lord came as a tender plant, and with no form nor comeliness, yet has He become a *"Plant of Renown,"* for already no other name is so widely known, no other name carries such wondrous power, no other name shows such boundless grace, and sometime, perhaps soon, "every knee shall bow and every tongue proclaim" that the Tender Plant is a Plant of Renown, that "Jesus Christ is Lord to the glory of God the Father."

Thou sawest till that a stone was cut out without hands, which smote the image upon his feet that were of iron and clay, and brake them to pieces. . .and the stone that smote the image became a great mountain, and filled the whole earth.

DANIEL 2:34–35

People plan for peace in human governments, build courts of arbitration, leagues of nations, pacts and pledges, only to find them crumbling in utter failure before the human work is half complete. The eternal God is planning a kingdom and government that cannot fail, and He the King, whose shape and form and size and power are ordered by the Most High God, will smite in His coming every man-made plan. Are we looking for that "Stone" to come and smite? Shall we be ready in the day of His power?

*I saw in the night visions, and, behold, one like the Son
of man came with the clouds of heaven, and came to
the Ancient of days, and they brought him near before
him. . . . His dominion is an everlasting dominion,
which shall not pass away, and his kingdom that which
shall not be destroyed.*

DANIEL 7:13–14

*I*n the beginning was the Word," and He who
redeemed us is the "Ancient of Days," whose head
is "white as snow" (Revelation 1:14). He was from
everlasting and will be unto the ages of ages our
eternal God. Shall not we, whose life upon the earth
is but a handbreadth, bow in worship and adoration
at the feet of the Ancient of Days?

He shall also stand up against the Prince of princes;
but he shall be broken without hand.

DANIEL 8:25

By every word that men could understand, Almighty God has sought to exalt His Son, so that in all things He might have the preeminence in our lives, as King of kings, as Lord of lords, and as in this text, as the "Prince of princes." In earthly kingdoms it is very often true that upon the prince who is heir apparent to the throne is lavished more affection than upon the king himself. What about our love and affection to the Prince of princes? Although sitting now at the right hand of the Father and one with Him, He is waiting to be crowned on earth. Do we pay Him more devotion and deeper love than we do to these erring mortals who reign over us? Let us, in the real things of daily life, exalt Him to His rightful place and pour out our devotion to Him.

> *The LORD also shall roar out of Zion, and utter his voice from Jerusalem; and the heavens and the earth shall shake: but the LORD will be the hope of his people, and the strength of the children of Israel.*
>
> JOEL 3:16

There is no hope apart from Him; no hope in self to win against the world, the flesh, and the devil! No hope in self to either be or do that which shall bless the world; but there is glorious hope for those who trust in Him. Jesus, who is our Savior, King, and Bridegroom, the living Head of the Body of which we are but humble members, is the "Hope of His People." He it is who "worketh in me both to will and to do."

> *But thou, Bethlehem Ephratah, though thou*
> *be little among the thousands of Judah, yet*
> *out of thee shall he come forth unto me that*
> *is to be ruler in Israel; whose goings forth*
> *have been from of old, from everlasting.*
> MICAH 5:2

*N*ever in the history of the world has there been such hopeless failure of human governments as now. Never such high ideals, and never have high ideals fallen so flat. Great plans are made and conferences held to promote peace and good government, and like flimsy houses of cards the highest hopes are shattered in ruthless, heartless, brutal war. So must it be until He who has the right to reign shall come and be "Ruler," not alone in Israel, but in all the world. More than thirty years ago one who was a chosen spokesman of the Lord said, "Perhaps He would have come sooner if we had, from our hearts, prayed more earnestly, 'Thy kingdom come.'" Do we ask it and sincerely desire it?

*The LORD is good, a strong hold in the day of trouble;
and he knoweth them that trust in him.*

NAHUM 1:7

During the late terrible war when the huge
flying craft sailed over London, multitudes of
people hid in the subways of London. In the
highlands of Central Africa there is a section
known as the "Iron Stone Plateau," where the
amount of ore appears to attract the lightning, and
many adventurers in that section, stopping long
at a place, dig cellars into which they go when
thunderstorms arise. There are dangerous storms
that beset our spiritual life from which there is no
safe retreat but Christ. Is He your "Stronghold"?
Have you learned to hide in Him?

> *For I, saith the LORD, will be unto her*
> *a wall of fire round about, and will*
> *be the glory in the midst of her.*
> ZECHARIAH 2:5

All the defense that we need is God to those who trust in Him. A "Wall of Fire" through which the fiercest foe can never come. The foe of evil thoughts will be burned. The hasty tongue will be consumed. The selfish desire that creeps so insidiously through every other barricade will be consumed by Him who is a Wall of Fire when we shall hide in Him.

Hear now, O Joshua the high priest, thou,
and thy fellows that sit before thee: for they
are men wondered at: for, behold, I will
bring forth my servant the BRANCH.
ZECHARIAH 3:8

*N*o lesson, not even that of courage, is more often repeated, and perhaps none is more often needed, than the lesson given us in our Lord's humility. He upon whose shoulders the Father laid all government; He who is the mighty God; He who, even when he subsisted "in the form of God," "made himself of no reputation" and became not only the Branch but "My Servant," and in doing this has marked the pathway for every child of God. Are you God's *servant*, serving Him as your only Master, doing joyfully and eagerly His will? If in aught you have sought to follow any other master, will you submit your life, your *all* to Him, and be His servant now?

And speak unto him, saying, Thus speaketh the L ORD of hosts, saying, Behold the man whose name is The B RANCH; and he shall grow up out of his place, and he shall build the temple of the L ORD.

ZECHARIAH 6:12

*W*hile He was here on earth *The Branch* said, "The Son can do nothing of himself, but what he seeth the Father do," taking the place of humility in His utter dependence upon God the Father. Are we tempted to exalt ourselves, to work in some strength that He has given in the past? Let us bow at His feet and remember that except we abide in Him, we can do nothing. Let us consider Him who, although He was the mighty God, yet called Himself in His earthly relationship "The Branch."

And his feet shall stand in that day upon the mount of Olives. . . . And the LORD my God shall come, and all the saints with thee. . . . And the LORD shall be king over all the earth: in that day shall there be one LORD, and his name one.

ZECHARIAH 14:4–5, 9

Someday, God grant it may be soon, His feet "shall stand upon the Mount of Olives," and all the earth shall know that He is King. Can any flight of swift imagination exceed that picture? Through all the strife of nations, all the pride and rivalry of kings, what peace, what glory, what undreamed-of wonders shall be seen when He, the King of kings, shall reign "over all the earth." Does that day not allure you? Does not the Spirit-given cry fill all your soul—"Even so, come, Lord Jesus!"

*And ye shall flee by the valley of my
mountains. . . . And Jehovah my God shall come,
and all the holy ones with thee.*
ZECHARIAH 14:5 ASV

*T*he Self-Existing One, seeking ever to reveal
Himself to His children and to the world that
knows Him not, is pleased and glorified when
that revelation leads our souls to cry, "Jehovah, my
God." If "that thing or person who most absorbs
our thought is our God," then who is my God
today? The matchless Jehovah? Or some other
being or created thing, unworthy of my trust and
worship? Let us not rest until from our inmost
soul we cry, "Jehovah, my God."

The King

And it shall come to pass, that every one that is left of all the nations which came against Jerusalem shall even go up from year to year to worship the King, the LORD of hosts, and to keep the feast of tabernacles.

ZECHARIAH 14:16

*H*e is King; it matters not that earth refused to crown Him and to acknowledge His right to reign. He only waits the Father's day and hour to receive the kingdom that is His. The world waits and weeps; the whole creation groans in pain for lack of the conditions that shall be when men and women have crowned Him King. We join that grief, but have we truly crowned Him in our lives? Does He reign supremely every day, in every act, and rule our words and thoughts? There will be joy in His heart, joy in heaven, and joy in your heart when you shall fully and with no reserve crown Jesus King and Lord of all.

Behold, I will send my messenger. . .even the messenger of the covenant, whom ye delight in: behold, he shall come, saith the LORD of hosts.

MALACHI 3:1

He who is our example that we should walk in His steps has called Himself the "Messenger of the Covenant." The Father gave a promise to those who should believe in His Son. The Son came bringing that promise, that covenant—a Messenger sent from heaven. To the true believer that most precious covenant is "I will write my laws upon their hearts, and upon their minds will I engrave them." Will you accept it now? "Open thy mouth wide, and I will fill it."

*And he shall sit as a refiner and purifier of silver:
and he shall purify the sons of Levi, and purge them
as gold and silver, that they may offer unto the LORD
an offering in righteousness.*

MALACHI 3:3

When grosser things that men and women can
see are removed from our lives, there is grave
danger that we shall be satisfied and forget that
still as the heaven is high above the earth, so high
are His ways above our ways, and His thoughts
above our thoughts. That there is a finer life, a
deeper, holier peace, a clearer, surer likeness of
the Lord possible for His children, needs to be
apprehended. And though through all of life
we may seem to have been in the melting pot,
shall we not say to Him again at any cost, "Dear
Refiner, make me what You will. Refine me by any
process that seems good to You."

Purifier

And he shall sit as a. . .purifier of silver.
MALACHI 3:3

*N*o work of God shows more plainly His boundless love than His desire to purify our lives. So much of dross is found in us that we have need to be tried in the furnace of affliction and to be purged as gold and silver. The difficult experiences through which we pass may often be understood as the infinite love of the Father, seeking to separate the dross from our lives, to bring us to a point of purity where we may see and reflect His image.

But unto you that fear my name shall the Sun of righteousness arise with healing in his wings.
MALACHI 4:2

*J*esus said, "When the Spirit of truth is come, he shall convince the world of righteousness, because I go to the Father." Among all humankind "there is none righteous, no, not one." But He who wrought in the creation of the worlds, and walked the streets of Judea, sits at the "right hand of the Father" in the glory. He is the Sun whose radiant righteousness heals our sin-sick souls. *Lord Jesus, we come with our earth stains and our innumerable faults and infirmities and bow at Your feet and worship You while we seek the healing in Your wings.*

The book of the generation of Jesus Christ.
MATTHEW 1:1

*H*ere is the first title given to our Lord in the New Testament—"Jesus Christ." This chapter contains a host of names, covering three periods of fourteen generations each, but one name stands out like a radiant star to lighten all the others; *one Person* to whom all must render allegiance—Jesus (Savior) Christ (the Anointed One). At His feet every knee shall bow in heaven and on earth. *Let us pour out our hearts to Him in praise and in prayer this day and every day. Amen.*

*The book of the generation of Jesus Christ,
the son of David.*

MATTHEW 1:1

*O*ur Lord was a lineal descendant of David, the
king. This entitled Him to the right of sovereignty
over David's land, and when He was here among
humankind, we are told, there was no other
claimant to the throne of David. Herod sought
to destroy the Child-King Jesus, but Egypt was
chosen as a refuge place for Him. The heart of
Herod was like the hearts of all people who will
not have Him to rule over them. He was bearing
us upon His heart as a child, for He is the same
"yesterday, today, and forever," and He is our
refuge now. *Jesus Christ, Son of David, may our
hearts be linked up with Your great heart always.
Amen.*

> *The book of the generation of Jesus Christ. . .*
> *the son of Abraham.*
>
> MATTHEW 1:1

*T*hree titles in one verse, "Jesus Christ—Son of David—Son of Abraham." Abraham was the head of the covenant nation. God had given to him the promise that in his seed should all the nations of the earth be blessed. Jesus submitted to the Jewish law in righteousness. He lived as a Jew; He preached to the Jews. He died for the Jews as well as for all people. "So then they which be of faith are blessed with faithful Abraham" (Galatians 3:9). How wonderful! God manifested in the flesh as Abraham's seed and yet the One who made the promise to Abraham! *Oh promised Son of Abraham and Son of God, our Savior, hold us fast in faith in Your Word. Amen.*

Thou shalt call his name JESUS: for he shall save his people from their sins.

MATTHEW 1:21

*O*ver seven hundred times in the New Testament is this name used—"Jesus" (Joshua). How familiar we are with that name! Joshua of the Old Testament, who saved Israel by leading them through the river Jordan, fought their battles, and was steadfast in his allegiance to God and His people. He was a type of our Lord who is our Joshua; who fights our battles for us; who is our Leader, our Protector, our Savior! Who will never cease His lordship until He has us safely in the sheepfold on the other side. Hallelujah, what a Savior! *This day, Savior of our souls, in whom we are separated for eternity, guide us by Your Holy Spirit to the praise of Your grace. Amen.*

Behold, a virgin. . .shall bring forth a son, and they shall call his name Emmanuel.

MATTHEW 1:23

*T*his was the prophecy of Isaiah 7:14: "Therefore the Lord himself shall give you a sign; Behold, a virgin shall conceive, and bear a son, and shall call his name Immanuel." "Emmanuel"—God with us! What a wonderful God and Savior He is, and He is with us as He promised in Matthew 28:19–20: "Go ye therefore, and teach all nations, baptizing them in the name of the Father, and of the Son, and of the Holy Ghost: Teaching them to observe all things whatsoever I have commanded you: and, lo, I am with you always, even unto the end of the world." Let us sense His presence and make Him real. Walk, talk, live with, and love Him more and more as the days go by. *Lord Jesus, we know that You dwell in us. May we enjoy Your fellowship today. Amen.*

*And thou Bethlehem. . .out of thee shall come a
Governor, that shall rule my people Israel.*
MATTHEW 2:6

Bethlehem of Judah! A little village, twice
highly honored! The birthplace of David, king
of Israel, and the birthplace of Jesus the Christ,
King of kings and Lord of lords! Who could visit
this land of promise and not desire to see this
city of cities, the place where Jehovah enthroned
in human form and lying in a manger gazed into
the face of the virgin Mary, His mother? The
government shall be upon His shoulders, and He
will reign in righteousness. Blessed day! *We pray
for its soon coming and ask for grace that we may
hasten it. Amen.*

*When they had heard the king, they departed;
and, lo, the star, which they saw in the east,
went before them, till it came and stood over where
the young child was.*

MATTHEW 2:9

A star in the East led the wise men to a Star
that shall outshine all the stars of heaven. Look at
this Young Child! Hold fast your attention as you
gaze upon His face, lying there, His eyes looking
into your own inquiring eyes. Visualize, if you can,
God manifested in the flesh for you. God—the
Young Child! The Creator of all things! Before
whom are thirty years of human life in which
He will toil with His fellow men. Mystery of
mysteries! *Oh Wonderful One, as we bow before You
today, help us to discern something of Your devotion to
humankind. Amen.*

And he came and dwelt in a city called Nazareth:
that it might be fulfilled which was spoken by the
prophets, He shall be called a Nazarene.
MATTHEW 2:23

*N*azareth was a town in the northern border
of the plain of Esdraelon. Here came the angel
Gabriel and announced to Mary the coming
birth of Christ: "And the angel came in unto her,
and said, Hail, thou that art highly favoured,
the Lord is with thee: blessed art thou among
women" (Luke 1:28). On the night of His betrayal
our Lord asked the question, "Whom do you
seek?" They replied, "Jesus of Nazareth," and He
said, "I am He." *Jesus of Nazareth, may we never*
be ashamed to be called the followers of the lowly
Nazarene.

Behold. . .a friend of publicans and sinners.
MATTHEW 11:19

*T*hese are the words of Jesus Himself. He quotes their own phrases as applied to Himself. What a title! How wonderfully true it is—a "Friend of Sinners"! So He was and so He is—a Friend who sticks closer than a brother. Laying aside the royal robes of heaven, he came here to befriend sinful people. It was a lifework that cost Him His life. Hallelujah! What a Friend! How gladly He paid the price of friendship. As we take up the work of the day, let us ask ourselves the question, "Am I a friend of sinners?" If not, then I am not like my Lord, for He was and He joyed in it. *Lord Jesus, the world is full of friendless sinners. May we make them acquainted with You, their Friend. Amen.*

Behold my servant, whom I have chosen.
MATTHEW 12:18

*J*esus, the prophesied Servant! Isaiah had portrayed Him. Jehovah had chosen Him. All of God's ways were known unto Him from the beginning. You hear the echo of His voice, "I delight to do Your will, oh my God!" Nothing was too great for Him to do, for He was the Creator, and nothing was too hard for Him, for He had all power. Nothing was too small for Him to do, for He stooped to notice a widow's mite and give a mighty lesson from it. What a gracious privilege to be yoked with Him in service. *Dear Lord, let us labor with You, the "Servant of Jehovah," today and thus make it a good day for You. Amen.*

My Beloved

Behold. . .my beloved, in whom
my soul is well pleased.

MATTHEW 12:18

*T*wenty-seven times in the Song of Solomon is this title used of our Lord. God's Son was a *beloved* Servant. How dear He was to the Father—dear as the apple of His eye. Yet His love for us was manifest in the surrender of His Son to pay the penalty of our sin. "Greater love hath no man than this." "While we were yet sinners, Christ died for us." In the hour of darkness He cried, "My God, my God, why hast thou forsaken me?" The agony, the grief, the pain He suffered, all had a voice that rings out the message "God so loved." *Our Father, Your love for us has broken all the barriers down, and we pray that Your Spirit may rest upon us this day as we meditate upon the greatness of Your love. Amen.*

He that soweth the good seed is the Son of man.
MATTHEW 13:37

The seed is the Word of God. God's Son sowed the good seed. He sows the Word of Truth in the hearts of men and women. When we sow the gospel, we sow good seed. When we give out the Word of God, we are sowing good seed. Nothing is comparable to the *Word* itself. It has potential power. It is a *living* seed and never fails. We are to imitate our Lord, the Sower, and see that the pure seed of the Word is scattered wherever we go. "Sow beside all waters." *Lord, make me a seed-sower this day, and hear my prayer for all the sowers in all the world. Amen!*

Thou art the Christ, the Son of the living God.
MATTHEW 16:16

This is the title of the long-looked-for Savior—the Anointed One. Prophets had foretold His coming, and now His kingly authority is recorded. Over three hundred times is this title used in the New Testament. From "Christ" comes the word "Christian," and from "Christian" comes the word "Christianity." Today this land of ours is the foremost Christian nation of the world. Our gospel is the gospel of Christ, of which we are not ashamed, for it is the power of God unto salvation to everyone who believes. *Lord, as "Christ-ones" let us honor You by having the same anointing power resting upon us as we enter the service of the day. Amen.*

Then charged he his disciples that they should tell no man that he was Jesus the Christ.
MATTHEW 16:20

*T*his title, "Jesus the Christ," is used a hundred times in the New Testament. "The Savior—the Anointed One"—a combination that magnifies the office of the One whom we long to worship. The time had not yet come for them to preach the story of redemption. They were to hold their peace for a season, but He tells us to go into all the world and tell all people the wonderful message of Jesus Christ and His finished work. Are we obeying the command? *Dear Father, as we go forth today with this precious name in our hearts and on our lips, help us to tell someone of the wonders of the Man, Your Son, Jesus the Christ! Amen.*

This is my beloved Son, in whom I am
well pleased; hear ye him.

MATTHEW 17:5

*W*onderful manifestation! A cloud of glory overshadowing that which was too deep for human eyes to penetrate. The voice of Jehovah attesting that Jesus was His beloved Son and that His words were to be heard. The same voice and the same message were heard in chapter 3, verse 17, when our Lord was baptized, and once again in John 12:28 in Jerusalem. His Beloved and our Beloved! How marvelous is that testimony to Him whom we have learned to love, and because we love Him, we are beloved of the Father. *Lord, may we breathe it over and over again today, "I am my Beloved's, and my Beloved is mine." Amen.*

This is Jesus the prophet of Nazareth of Galilee.
MATTHEW 21:11

*T*his great demonstration had been planned by God and foretold by Him (Zechariah 9:9). Our Lord comes into Jerusalem riding upon the foal of a donkey. The crowd is vast; the enthusiasm is great. "Who is this?" is the cry; and the answer is, "This is Jesus, the Prophet of Nazareth." A despised Nazarene! A prophet from an obscure village! We are all proud if, perchance, we were born in some noted place; but God, when He took the form of a man, was born in a manger and made His home in Nazareth. For our sakes He became poor, that we through His poverty might be made rich. *Let us meditate upon the riches of His grace, bow at His feet and kiss them as we adore Him; and may we walk humbly this day with the despised Nazarene. Amen.*

Master

*One is your Master, even Christ; and all
ye are brethren.*

MATTHEW 23:8

*M*aster" here means "Teacher," or some say,
"Leader." The admonition is to avoid the desire
for personal distinction so common among God's
leaders. Let our eyes be fixed upon Him, and let
us depend upon the Holy Spirit who represents
Him and who guides us into all truth (John
16:13–14). The more we seek to exalt Him, the
less will we think of magnifying ourselves. Make
Him Master of your life today, remembering that
"the disciple is not above his master: but every
one that is perfect shall be as his master" (Luke
6:40). *Oh, that we may be as our Master, the meek
and lowly One! For this day, our Lord, we need great
grace as we seek to follow You as Master. Amen.*

And while they went to buy, the bridegroom came.
MATTHEW 25:10

The Bridegroom must come. The true church is
His beloved espoused bride. He has waited a long,
long time for her to prepare herself for the glad
day and to add the last one who will complete
the body. Are you thinking of Him today as the
Coming One? And of yourself as one of those
who is to be blessed as His beloved throughout
eternity? How insignificant are all the little cares
and trials! How small they seem when our eyes
are turned with expectancy toward Him as He
comes in the clouds. "Blessed are they which are
called unto the marriage supper of the Lamb"
(Revelation 19:9). Hallelujah! May our prayer
always be, "Even so, come, Lord Jesus, come
quickly." Amen.

I know thee who thou art, the Holy One of God.
MARK 1:24

What a testimony coming from the lips of one possessed of an unclean spirit, Satan's tool, under his power. But the presence of Christ overawed him. "I know thee who thou art, the Holy One of God." This was not a willing testimony but was forced from him. Many men are devil-possessed, and the devil has powers accorded him, but Christ can hinder his followers; can cast out his demons and forbid their speaking (verse 34). How lovingly we should bow at His feet—the Holy One of God! May we fix our thoughts upon Him and say many times today as we walk and talk with Him, "Oh Holy One of God, glorify Yourself through us." Amen.

*For whosoever shall do the will of God,
the same is my brother.*

MARK 3:35

*I*f this is true, and it is, then the reverse is
also true, and He is our Brother. The picture
is given in the thirty-first and thirty-fourth
verses: "There came then his brethren and his
mother, and, standing without, sent unto him,
calling him. . . . And he looked round about on
them which sat about him, and said, Behold my
mother and my brethren!" How wonderful that
He should graciously give this title to those who
do the Father's will! And what is that will? The
acceptance of His Son as our Savior and Lord,
and the submission of our will to His will as
revealed in His Word, for His Word is His will.
How near and dear He is to us, our Lord and our
Brother! Hold it fast in your meditation—"Ours
by faith; ours forever." *Dear Lord, keep us in loving
fellowship with Thyself this day. Amen.*

*And cried with a loud voice, and said, What
have I to do with thee, Jesus, thou Son of
the most high God?*

MARK 5:7

*H*ere we are confronted with another
testimony from an unclean spirit—"Son of the
Most High God," he calls Jesus. What unseen
powers compelled this significant title? Was
it brought about by being face-to-face with
Himself? Judas betrayed Him, but this poor
demon-possessed man worshipped Him. In
these strange days many teachers, professors, and
preachers refuse to honor Him as the Son, but
only as a Son of God. But we lift our hearts to
Him and say, "*Son of the Most High God, be our
companion this day, and may we withhold nothing
from You.*" Amen.

The Carpenter

Is not this the carpenter?

MARK 6:3

*T*he Carpenter! Two things are suggested in this verse. Joseph is not mentioned and is probably not now living. Jesus is working at the carpenter's bench and continued to do so until He assumed His place in His public ministry. We can and should visualize Him in His daily tasks—a man among men. How near He seems to us! What a joy to know that He handled the hammer and sharpened the saw, planed the plank, and helped to supply the food for the family. Test this picture of Him with any false system and observe the contrast. No matter what our calling may be, the Carpenter will be one with us. We can walk arm in arm with Him to the daily task. *Oh Carpenter of Galilee, be our ideal always! Amen.*

The Son of Mary

Is not this. . .the son of Mary?

MARK 6:3

The Carpenter, the "Son of Mary," has come back to His hometown from an evangelistic trip in which He had worked many miracles. The people were astonished at His teaching. Prejudice possessed them. "Is not this the Son of Mary?" We never worship Mary as do our Catholic friends, but we do honor her above all women—God's chosen vessel to bring forth His Son and fulfill His prophecy. How true He was to the last. See Him on the cross and hear His last words to Mary, "Woman, behold thy son" (John, the beloved, to whom He had said, "Behold thy mother"). *Blessed title—"Son of Mary"! The Babe who is one day to rule the world and at whose feet we shall bow in worshipful adoration! Let us do so now. Amen.*

*Good Master, what shall I do that
I may inherit eternal life?*

MARK 10:17

*T*his question was asked of our Lord by a young
man with great possessions, as recorded in Matthew
19:17. This is the concrete question of the soul of
man, "What shall I do to secure a right to heaven?"
The theme of religion is do; but the theme of our
Lord was just the opposite, "Follow Me." Eternal life
is a gift. Those who accept and follow Him find that
He is the "Good Master" because He is the "God-
Master," for only One is good and He is God, and
He has provided for us a salvation—simple to accept
but costing Him a price that involved His own life.
How gracious is our God, and how we should love
and adore Him! *Lord, may we walk in the sunshine of
Your love today. Amen.*

The Son of man shall be delivered unto the chief priests, and unto the scribes; and they shall condemn him to death.

MARK 10:33

*I*n the ninth chapter Jesus had said, "The Son of man is delivered into the hands of men, and they shall kill him." How earnestly He sought to stress the fact of His approaching sacrifice upon His disciples and how He longed for their sympathy; but alas, alas, how hard is the human heart! How difficult it is for Him to win us to Himself! "The Son of Man must suffer many things," He had said, but the saddest of all was the failure of His own beloved disciples to enter into the burden He bore as He approached the cross. *Oh holy Son of Man, give unto us the loving hearts that will enter into fellowship with You in all things. Amen.*

> *The Son of man came. . .to give his life*
> *a ransom for many.*
>
> MARK 10:45

"A ransom for many"! Here Christ is set forth as the penalty paid for the sins of the world. As we were sinners under the judgment wrath of God, He took our place and paid the penalty and the price of our deliverance with His own blood. Listen to the drops of blood as they fall from hands and feet and wounded side! They voice the words, "The ransom price for my sins and for the sins of the whole world." Would that men and women everywhere would believe it and receive it. How dear, how precious is He to us, washed clean in His blood and freed forever from the punishment due us. *Lord, may our ransomed souls well up in praise to Your glorious name! Amen.*

Having yet therefore one son, his wellbeloved,
he sent him also last unto them, saying,
They will reverence my son.

MARK 12:6

The Savior is in Jerusalem. The chief priests and scribes come to Him and question His authority. Jesus answers them in the parable of the vineyard, picturing to them the treatment of the servants who were sent to gather the fruit, telling the story—so old, so strange—of the attitude of the human heart toward God. He sent His Son, His well-beloved Son, and they took Him and killed Him and cast Him out. How could they? They have cast Him out of the schools and many of the churches, though all we have of earthly civilization and comforts today we owe to Him. *God's well-beloved Son, we enthrone You today in our hearts. Help us to worship and adore You. Amen.*

Art thou the Christ, the Son of the Blessed?
MARK 14:61

*T*he court is convened. The high priest is presiding. Charges had been brought against the Lord Jesus Christ by false witnesses, but they had not agreed. The high priest put to Him a question: "Art thou the Christ, the Son of the Blessed?" And He answered, "I am." There was no denial of the title, but a straight confession of His sonship, heirship, power, and coming glory. And when He comes—if He tarries yet a season—we will be among those who will be caught up in the clouds to meet Him in the air and with the hosts of heaven acclaim Him "Blessed"! *Lord Jesus Christ, Son of the Blessed, hasten the glad day. Amen.*

And Pilate asked him, Art thou the King of the Jews?
And he answering said unto them, Thou sayest it.
MARK 15:2

What a title for our Lord to put His seal upon
at the time when the Jews were in subjection to
the Romans and He Himself a prisoner before a
judge. But He is King of the Jews—yes, *King of
kings and Lord of all.* Pilate will yet stand before
Him to be judged, and the Jewish people will yet
proclaim Him as their own King. He is the Ruler.
Let us give Him His rightful place as Ruler in
our lives. How can we serve Him today? Perhaps
in some definite prayer for the Jewish people and
some testimony to them of the joy there is in
knowing, loving, and serving Him. *Lord, remember
Your ancient people and all who seek to make You
known to them. Amen.*

*He shall be great, and shall be called
the Son of the Highest.*

LUKE 1:32

*T*his is the message of the angel to Mary, and here is a remarkable coincidence. In Mark 5:7, we have the evil spirit in the man in the tombs giving a similar title to Jesus, "Son of the most high God." The title here given Him is in fulfillment of Psalm 132:11: "The LORD hath sworn in truth unto David; he will not turn from it; of the fruit of thy body will I set upon thy throne." David's heir is to reign as Son of the Most High God, and that time only waits for the completion of the church that is His body. Let us do our best each day to win souls for Him and thus hasten the day when we shall be with Him and reign with Him. *Son of the Highest, we bow to You; we worship You. Help us to magnify Your name today. Amen.*

And my spirit hath rejoiced in God my Saviour.
LUKE 1:47

The word "Savior" here is "Soter," meaning "presence." Should we not imitate Mary, the blessed woman, in magnifying our Savior and rejoicing in the finished work that He has wrought in our behalf? It is never what we are but what He is. Our joy is in Him, and we rejoice with joy unspeakable and full of glory as we face this day with joyful hearts. Shall we not have a tender heart for those who do not know Him? *Savior, like a shepherd lead us today to glorify Your name in our efforts to win souls for You. Amen.*

*And hath raised up an horn of salvation
for us in the house of his servant David.*
LUKE 1:69

*H*ere is a title that suggests the strength and
power of our Lord—"Horn of Salvation." The
word "horn" as used in the scripture signifies
"strength" and is often found in Hebrew literature.
In the horns, the bull manifests his strength.
The Lord Jesus Christ is our Strength and a very
present help in time of trouble (Psalms 28:7;
37:39; 92:10; 118:14). "But the salvation of the
righteous is of the LORD; he is their strength in
the time of trouble." You may be tempted and
tried today. You may have burdens to bear. Let
Him be your "Horn of Salvation." *Lord, strengthen
us by the power of Your might for today's service for
You. Amen.*

*And thou, child, shalt be called
the prophet of the Highest.*

LUKE 1:76

*L*isten to the voice of Zacharias, father of John the Baptist, as he voices the wonderful prophecy concerning his son, who was to be the prophet of the Lord to prepare the way before Him. Our Lord is here named the "Highest" or, better, the "Most High." He came from the heights of glory to be born in a manger. "Prophet" in the New Testament means a "public expounder" and to us, His redeemed ones, has been committed this honorable title. We are the expounders of this great revelation of the Bible concerning our most highly exalted Lord. *Glory to God in the highest, King of kings and Lord of lords, whom we claim as our own. Amen.*

*Through the tender mercy of our God; whereby the
dayspring from on high hath visited us.*

LUKE 1:78

Zacharias is inspired as his soul goes forth
to speak of the coming of the Messiah. It has
been suggested that the glory of the sunrise was
breaking over the hills surrounding Jerusalem,
and the golden glory lit up the horizon as his
lips breathed the words inspired by the Spirit
of God, "Dayspring from on high!" Perhaps the
morning glory brought to the mind of Zacharias
the message of Isaiah, "Arise, shine, for thy light
is come, and the glory of the LORD is risen upon
thee." *Before we take up our daily tasks, let us turn
our eyes to the heavens with grateful hearts and let the
Holy Spirit flood our souls with the glory of the risen,
coming Christ. Amen.*

For unto you is born this day in the city of David a Saviour, which is Christ the Lord.

LUKE 2:11

*T*he heavens are opened now, and the message of the angel of the Lord is announced—"good tidings of great joy." The message was to the humble shepherds, and it will mean much to us if we can, in humility of heart, take our place with the shepherds, acknowledge our unworthiness, and appropriate the truth to our own souls— "Unto you is born a Saviour, which is Christ the Lord" (the Anointed One—the Ruler). We are no longer to rule ourselves. He is to rule us. *Lord, with joy we submit our wills and surrender all to You. Help us to magnify You this day. Amen.*

Ye shall find the babe wrapped in swaddling clothes, lying in a manger.

LUKE 2:12

*A*gain the voice of the angel rings out to the shepherds: "Christ the Lord—the Babe—lying in a manger." How easy it would be for the shepherds to find Him. No other newly born babe would be found "lying in a manger"—just One—and He, the altogether lovely One, the chiefest among ten thousand! Sometimes the saints magnify their human birthright and place of birth, but He was to be a blessing to the humblest. Would not the cattle—could they have sensed the significance of the event—have bent their knees in homage to the Babe? How sad to know that millions in our land have not yet bowed the knee to Him. *Lord, may we who have named Your name bow in humblest submission to You today and pour out our hearts in joyful praise to You, Babe of Bethlehem. Amen.*

> *There was a man in Jerusalem, whose name was*
> *Simeon; and the same man was just and devout,*
> *waiting for the consolation of Israel.*
>
> LUKE 2:25

*S*imeon was just and devout and waited for the "Consolation of Israel." "Consolation" means "paraclete" (one coming alongside) as we think and speak of the Holy Spirit who comes to abide in and lead us out in our daily life. Simeon was waiting for the deliverance of the Jews by the coming of the Messiah. They did not as a nation receive Him, but some did and were consoled, and Israel shall yet have the promised consolation, as Paul was comforted by the power of the indwelling Holy Spirit (1 Thessalonians 1:5). *Lord, may we also rely upon the abiding comfort of the indwelling of the Holy Spirit all the day. Amen.*

*And it was revealed unto him by the Holy Ghost,
that he should not see death, before
he had seen the Lord's Christ.*

LUKE 2:26

Simeon was a just and devout man who
believed the Word of God and rested upon its
promises. The Holy Ghost came upon him and
made a revelation to him. He was not to taste of
death until he had tasted the sweets of seeing and
knowing the "Lord's Christ." The Lord never fails
His loved ones. When He can get hold of the
hearts of men and women, He is glad to make a
revelation of Himself to them and give unto them
the power of the Holy Spirit. His great heart beats
in sympathy with every loyal-hearted follower.
*Holy Spirit, give us new spiritual visions of the Lord's
Christ. Amen.*

For mine eyes have seen thy salvation.

LUKE 2:30

*T*he aged saint Simeon, standing in the temple, took the child Jesus in his arms and, looking into His face, lifted his eyes to heaven and said, "Lord, now lettest thou thy servant depart in peace, according to thy word; for *mine eyes have seen thy salvation.*" Long had he waited, long had he prayed, long had he desired to see Him. Now the Spirit of God revealed unto him the fact that his heart's desire had been granted and that he was gazing upon the divine Savior of souls and death had no more terrors for him. There is but one cure for the world's unrest, the "Salvation of God." Let us go out today and tell the story wherever we can. The poor, hungry-hearted, sin-sick souls are waiting. *Lord, guide us in this service to Your glory. Amen.*

A light to lighten the Gentiles, and the glory of thy people Israel.

LUKE 2:32

*T*he world has been a dark world ever since Adam and Eve listened to the temptation of Satan. There was no hope until God said, "The seed of the woman shall bruise the serpent's head"—a promise of coming victory for a lost race. He who is the Light of the Gentiles is the Light of the world (Matthew 4:16). The Light shone for Israel first, but Israel rejected its blessed beams. But again the Light shall shine for the people now wandering over the earth in darkness. What is the duty of believers? Is it not to lift the Light high so that the world of sinners in darkness may come into fellowship with Him? *Lord of Light, help us to shine as lights in a dark world this day. Amen.*

> *A light to lighten the Gentiles,*
> *and the glory of thy people Israel.*
>
> LUKE 2:32

*T*he message of Paul was "to the Jew first," but here the Gentiles are mentioned first. The Jews turned away from Jesus and would not have Him to rule over them, but the Gentiles will not receive Him, either—just a few. The glory shall rest upon Israel when He comes with scepter in hand to rule a reconstructed earth. The Shekinah glory, manifested in the tabernacle and temple, will shine again upon His beloved people, and Jesus—the Jew—will be the glory of Israel in that day. Let us love the Jews and seek to bring the gospel of the grace of God to them. *Lord Jesus, the "Glory of Thy People Israel," remember Your persecuted, penalty-paying people and help us to love them. Amen.*

*This child is set. . .for a sign which
shall be spoken against.*

LUKE 2:34

Our Lord Jesus Christ was a significant sign to
Israel. The prophecies had long before made clear
that Israel was to be tested when the Messiah
came. Some would believe and follow Him. Some
would reject and crucify Him. Our Lord gave
testimony to this fact when Pilate asked Him,
"Art thou a King?" And His answer was: "To
this end was I born, and for this cause came I
into the world." Poor Pilate, he had his evidence
but would not accept it. Where is he? The Sign
has been given to our land also. Where are the
multitudes? The same old story will be told again
and again. *Oh Lord, have compassion upon this poor
land. Inspire Your servants to be brave and true in
sounding the alarm. Amen.*

The child Jesus tarried behind in Jerusalem.
LUKE 2:43

*H*ere we have our first view of Jesus as a young lad, interested in the business of His heavenly Father. Hear Him when Joseph and Mary seek Him: "Wist ye not that I must be about my Father's business?" The strangeness of the story of His life is a constant surprise. God manifested in the flesh—a Child—with words of wisdom falling from His lips—a message for us all, "Occupy [do business] till I come." Every disciple is a businessman or -woman, and our business is the most important in all the world. Let us take as a motto for our daily life the words of the Child Jesus, "I must be about my Father's business." *Lord, help us to be busy about Your business this day. Amen.*

> *And he said unto them, Ye will surely say unto me this proverb, Physician, heal thyself.*
>
> LUKE 4:23

*O*ur Lord had been in Galilee. His fame had spread throughout that region. He had wrought mighty miracles. He comes back home to Nazareth where He had been brought up and preaches in the synagogue on the Sabbath day from Isaiah 61:1–3, saying, "This day is this scripture fulfilled in your ears." The people who heard these words said, "Is not this Joseph's son?" and then Jesus quoted to them our verse, a proverb among the Jews. What a mistake they made. He *was* the Great Physician. He *is* the Great Physician—"able to do exceeding abundantly above all that we ask or think." How few know Him as such a One! How few look to Him! How few depend upon Him! *Lord, You who are the Great Physician, we look to You today to supply our every need. Amen.*

And he said unto them, That the Son of man is Lord also of the sabbath.

LUKE 6:5

He is the Master (Lord) of the Sabbath. He is the Maker of heaven and earth. "Without him nothing was made that is made." He is either what He claimed to be, or else He is the greatest impostor who ever lived. The Sabbath was made for man, and not man for the Sabbath. It is lawful to do good on the Sabbath. Serving others is serving the Lord of the Sabbath. He, with His disciples, plucked and ate the wheat on the Sabbath, and on the Sabbath He healed the man with the withered hand. The Sabbath is the Lord's day. Solve all your problems in connection with the Sabbath day by the question, "What would the Lord do on this day?" Then whatever you do, whether you eat or drink, do all to the glory of God. *Lord Jesus, we pray that every day may be a good day for You through our lives. Amen.*

And they glorified God, saying, That a great prophet is risen up among us; and, That God hath visited his people.

LUKE 7:16

*F*our centuries had elapsed since Malachi had passed away, and Israel had been without a prophetic voice. Now they are stirred by the presence of Jesus and glorify God. Israel was not forsaken. God's Word was true. And Jesus was a great Prophet; yes, greater even than they knew. Humble, quiet, gentle, no pomp, no display, but wonderful in works. Do we recognize His greatness? Do we believe His prophecies and promises? Do we possess them and profit by them and give glory to His name? *Lord, help us to believe every word of the Prophetic Book. Amen.*

> *He said unto them, But whom say ye that I am?*
> *Peter answering said, The Christ of God.*
>
> LUKE 9:20

*J*esus was alone in prayer and asked His disciples the question, "Whom say the people that I am?" and after they had given their answers, He asked the question in our text. The disciples were compelled to recognize His heavenly gifts, His greatness, His power, and His gracious Spirit, but it was hard for them to think of Him as One who must suffer persecution and death at the hands of the Jews. But He knew all that was before Him and walked steadily on toward the cruel cross upon which He must die. Today the *professing* church is inclined to reject the theme of His atoning blood, but those of us to whom He is the "Christ of God" adore Him more and more as the depths of His sacrifice and suffering are revealed. *Lord, may we hold Thee in our hearts today as "the Christ of God." Amen.*

> *But a certain Samaritan, as he journeyed. . .*
> *had compassion on him.*
>
> LUKE 10:33

The story of the Good Samaritan is familiar to all of us, but read it again. Here we take the liberty of viewing our Lord as "a certain Samaritan." Humanity was His neighbor. He loved all, lived for all, labored for all, and laid down His life for all. Being what He was and is, He could be nothing less, and we look up to Him today and glory in the mightiness of His humanity and the magnificence of His heart. If we are indeed Spirit-born, then there must be something of His loving-kindness in us, and the world is waiting for our touch upon it. Will we take the Good Samaritan for our model today and pray, "*Lord Jesus, make us more like Yourself*"? Amen.

The Master of the House

When once the master of the house is risen up...
he shall answer and say unto you,
I know you not whence ye are.

LUKE 13:25

*H*ere is a new title for our Lord—"Master of the House." How appropriate it is—"Lord of the house—the Head—the Governor." The "house" is heaven where He is to rule. The appeal is for earnest effort upon the part of believers to impress upon the unsaved the fact that there is a heaven and there is a hell, and only one gate to heaven— Jesus Christ. Why do we not make more definite to people the awful consequences of failure to hear His voice now, and that there will come a time when it will be too late? *Dear Lord, may we labor and pray earnestly today that we may be faithful in urging upon people the necessity of decision for Christ. Amen.*

And when they saw it, they all murmured,
saying, That he was gone to be guest
with a man that is a sinner.

LUKE 19:7

*Z*acchaeus was highly honored when Christ invited Himself to be his guest. How like our Lord! He knew Zacchaeus wanted to see Him, and He sought him out and became his guest. How we would congratulate ourselves were some noted person to come to our house to dine. What a fuss we would make. How we would boast about it. Why do we not tell the story to everybody, "A Great One has come to live in my house?" "Who is He?" "He is the King of glory. He holds the worlds in the hollow of His hand. He lives with me." *Oh blessed Guest, help us today to magnify and glorify You before all. Amen.*

> *He said therefore, A certain nobleman went*
> *into a far country to receive for himself*
> *a kingdom, and to return.*
>
> LUKE 19:12

*T*he setting of this picture is remarkable. Our
Lord is standing with the Jews around Him
in the shadow of a palace built by a nobleman,
Archelaus, who had gone to Rome and received
the kingdom from Caesar. Our Lord is the
Nobleman whose face was turned toward the
land beyond the skies where He has gone and
from whence He will one day return. "Occupy
till I come" is His message. He has entrusted to
us, as His servants, the most valuable treasures of
heaven—time, opportunity, the gifts of the Holy
Spirit, a great wide world in which to transact the
greatest of all business! Precious privileges are ours
and a solemn accounting must be given. *Lord, give
us keenness of vision to see and wisdom to utilize our
opportunities in the investment of our lives for You.
Amen.*

> *Let him save himself, if he be Christ,*
> *the chosen of God.*
>
> LUKE 23:35

*C*hrist is on the cross. He prays, "Father, forgive them." The people stand beholding Him; the rulers deride Him and mock Him. What a picture! What a slur! "*If* thou be the Christ, the *chosen of God*"? So do men and women today. The question mark grows as the days go by, but the title that was given Him in derision is a wonderfully true one and is found again in 1 Peter 2:4. Yes, indeed! Chosen before the foundation of the earth, and the *only One* who could be chosen for the great work of our redemption. *Lord, You have chosen Him, and You have chosen us. May we adore and glory in You this day. Amen.*

A Prophet Mighty in Deed and Word

And he said unto them, What things? And they said unto him, Concerning Jesus of Nazareth, which was a prophet mighty in deed and word before God and all the people.

LUKE 24:19

Some hated Him. Some worshipped Him. Mighty in life, mighty in death, and mighty in His resurrection! The rulers thought they had eliminated Him. Some seek to do so today. They crucified Him in fulfillment of scripture, but He is alive today. He lives in the hearts of millions who would be willing to be crucified for Him. He will live throughout the eternal ages, and every word He ever uttered will be fulfilled to the letter. *Oh mighty Prophet, help us to lay hold of the Word with intensified faith and hold fast until You shall come. Amen.*

The Word

In the beginning was the Word, and the
Word was with God, and the Word was God.
JOHN 1:1

*W*e come today to John's Gospel, in which we shall find many titles for the Son of God. Here we confront the first—the "Word." The book of Genesis commences with creation, but John commences with the Creator. Back of all things with which we ever have had or will have to do is *the Word*. "The Word was God"! What a foundation for our faith when we know that Jesus was the Word and the Word was God. Every day we can, if we will, be facing this tremendous fact, and as we feel the throb of our heart, there is a voice that says, "God!" As we look upon the heavens and the clouds—"God!" The sun, the moon, the trees, the flowers, the living creatures, all are saying, "God!" Without Him—nothing! With Him—all things! *Oh Living Word, who has given us the written Word, help us to abide in You today. Amen.*

In him was life; and the life was the light of men.
JOHN 1:4

od said, Let there be light: and there was
light" (Genesis 1:3). All life proceeds from our
Lord, and all light, also. The Word is a life- and
light-giving Word—"The light of the world is
Jesus." Visualize the whole world in the darkness
of sin, men and women groping blindly, restless
and hopeless. *We* have the Light of life. *We* see
Him face-to-face. *We* bask in the sunshine of His
glory. Pity the blind! Pray for the blind! Carry
the light of the glorious gospel to their darkened
souls. Tell them to arise and shine, for the Light is
come and the glory of the Lord shall shine upon
them. *Help us, Lord, to walk in the light as we have
fellowship with You and with one another. Amen.*

The True Light

That was the true Light, which lighteth every man that cometh into the world.

JOHN 1:9

"The true Light." This is in contrast with false lights. How many there are in our day. Satan is busy sending them forth through false cults, false teachers, and false teaching. False lights dazzle the eyes but never reveal truth, nor bring radiance to the soul. The gloom of sin, the uncertainty of life, the dark outlook for the future, confront the sinner stumbling along without God and without hope. God has ordained us as lights. Let our lights shine today, and may we help some blinded ones to see Jesus as the true Light of the world. *Lord Jesus, in the light of Your Word, and in the light of Yourself, may we witness for You today. Amen.*

And the Word was made flesh, and dwelt among us, (and we beheld his glory, the glory as of the only begotten of the Father,) full of grace and truth.
JOHN 1:14

This is the most sublime of all the statements of scripture—God became flesh! John saw His glory. How wonderful! That glory was manifest in the person of the Only Begotten of the Father—Jesus Christ. He is the Unique Figure in the world's history—the sinless, perfect One—perfect God and perfect Man. "Great is the mystery of godliness; God was manifest in the flesh." He must be God to forgive sin, and He must be Man to atone for sin. So the God-Man is our Savior. *We worship You, we adore You, oh Only Begotten of the Father. Help us to walk and talk with You this day. Amen.*

*The next day John seeth Jesus coming unto him,
and saith, Behold the Lamb of God, which
taketh away the sin of the world.*

JOHN 1:29

*H*ow shall we say in a few words that which springs up in our hearts and would break forth from our lips? "The Lamb which beareth away our sin" is a better rendering, for He takes it away by *bearing* it. He *bore* the sins of those who received Him while here on the earth, and He bore them *away* when He paid the penalty on the cross and shed His atoning blood. God's Lamb! No one else could be God's Lamb. He was the *voluntary* offering. What can we do? Believe it, accept it, take our place with Him. *Let us behold You every day—Jesus, Lamb of God—counting nothing too good to give to You or too much to do for You. Amen.*

*And I saw, and bare record that
this is the Son of God.*

JOHN 1:34

*J*ohn had not known Him as the Messiah,
although he did know Him to be Mary's son. But
when the Holy Spirit descended upon Jesus at
His baptism, John knew Him as the Son of God
and bore record to the fact. The testimony of
John the Baptist is clear! Jesus is God's Son. He
is the Promised One. Not *a* Son of God, as some
of our learned critics condescendingly say, but *the*
Son of God. We should seek to be like John the
Baptist—a signpost pointing to Him and saying,
"Behold! the Son of God." John laid down his
life for his loyalty to the Son of God. May we be
willing to suffer anything so that our testimony
shall be clear and clean always for Him. *Lord, help
us to point someone to You today. Amen.*

Rabbi

Nathanael answered and saith unto him, Rabbi,
thou art the Son of God; thou art the King of Israel.
JOHN 1:49

*R*abbi" means "teacher" and is used seven times
in the New Testament. Nathanael recognized
Christ as a teacher, and He was—the greatest
Teacher who ever lived. A careful study of the
four Gospels with a view to learning how Christ
taught, His method, His manner, and His
purpose, is better than any other possible training
for Bible teachers. Christ was a true teacher. He
taught the truth. He condescended to people
of low estate. He used words that people could
understand. He illustrated His messages in a
practical manner. "The common people heard him
gladly." That was a high compliment indeed. *Lord,*
help us to teach by our lips and by our life. Let us pray
that we may so teach today. Amen.

The King of Israel

*Nathanael answered and saith unto him,
Rabbi. . .thou art the King of Israel.*
JOHN 1:49

When Philip found Nathanael, the latter
said to him, "Can any good thing come out of
Nazareth?" But when Nathanael came in touch
with Jesus, he broke out in testimony to His deity
and His messiahship. Our Lord did not fail to
acknowledge this sterling testimony, and a great
promise was given to Nathanael: "Hereafter you
shall see heaven open, and the angels of God
ascending and descending." Ministering spirits
were to be seen by him. Prayers were to ascend
in the name of Christ and answers were to come
back through Christ. We also can see the open
heavens if we have faith. *Let us send up our prayers
today in His name and look for the answer. Amen.*

For God so loved the world, that he gave his only begotten Son, that whosoever believeth in him should not perish, but have everlasting life.

JOHN 3:16

*H*ere is the most beloved verse in the Bible. What a revelation of God, of Christ, of the depths and power of love! How could He? Abraham gave his son, and God graciously gave him back. But God's Son—the Son of His love—the Only Begotten One—was given to a lost world, to sinful humankind. How did He give Him? Clothed in human form—a Man! Oh, the wonders of such a love! How it should stir our hearts! How we should love God for His gift! How we should love our Lord Jesus Christ—God's only begotten Son! *Let us with throbbing hearts for a lost world go forth today, and all the days, to tell the story to sinful, suffering men and women. Amen.*

The woman saith unto him, I know that Messias cometh, which is called Christ: when he is come, he will tell us all things.

JOHN 4:25

*T*here is no book like the Bible, and there never can be. Christ's interview with the woman at the well and His revelation of Himself is unique and contrary to any conception that could have been made of Him. The Samaritans, as did the Jews, anticipated a Christ (an Anointed One). This was the promise given in Deuteronomy 18:18. This woman was the last one we would have chosen for such a revelation—but her soul was filled at once with the Spirit of life and hope, and her lips bore a testimony—humiliating to herself—but bringing salvation to a multitude. Oh, that our lips might bear such convincing, convicting, and converting testimony. *Lord, make us like this Samaritan woman! Amen.*

INDEX